GROWING GILLS

GROWING GILLS

A Fly Fisherman's Journey

David Joy

Illustrated by
Michael Polomik

Bright Mountain Books, Inc.
Fairview, North Carolina

Printed in the United States of America
ISBN-10: 0-914875-60-4 (paperback)
ISBN-13: 978-0-914875-60-4 (paperback)
ISBN-10: 0-914875-61-2 (E-book edition)
ISBN-13: 978-0-914875-61-1 (E-book edition)

Watercolor used on cover and illustrations by Michael Polomik
Cover design by Derek Howell and Jamie Womack

Slightly different versions of the following chapters have previously appeared in other publications: "Breaking in the Cork." *Wilderness House Literary Review* 4, no. 1 (Spring 2009): 1–9; "Native." *Smoky Mountain Living*, Summer 2009: 54–56; "Sound of Silence." *Smoky Mountain Living*, Winter 2010: 42–45.

Library of Congress Cataloging-in-Publication Data

Joy, David, 1983-
Growing gills : a fly fisherman's journey / David Joy.
p. cm.
Summary: "David Joy's Southern memoir details a North Carolina fly fisherman's youthful experiences in the Outer Banks and Piedmont to his pursuit of native brook trout in the Appalachian Mountains. This work of literary nonfiction encapsulates the philosophical underpinnings of a man defined by fish, family, water, solitude, environment, and wilderness"--Provided by publisher.
ISBN-13: 978-0-914875-60-4 (pbk. : alk. paper)
ISBN-10: 0-914875-60-4 (pbk. : alk. paper)
ISBN-13: 978-0-914875-61-1 (e-book ed.)
ISBN-10: 0-914875-61-2 (e-book ed.)
1. Joy, David, 1983- 2. Brook trout fishing--Appalachian Region. 3. Fly fishing--Appalachian Region. 4. Wilderness areas--Appalachian Region. 5. Fishers--Appalachian Region--Biography. 6. Fishers--North Carolina--Outer Banks--Biography. 7. Fishers--Piedmont (U.S. : Region)--Biography. 8. Appalachian Region--Social life and customs. 9. Outer Banks (N.C.)--Social life and customs. 10. Piedmont (U.S. : Region)--Social life and customs. I. Title.

SH689.3.J69 2011
799.17'554097568--dc23

2011032877

DEDICATION

To Granny, Ruth Weaver, who took me to the shoreline and taught me the ways of fish. Through her love, lessons of life, and stories of water, I find the courage to wade into the stream and face the current.

As the shadow of the kingfisher moved up the stream, a big trout shot upstream in a long angle, only his shadow marking the angle, then lost his shadow as he came through the surface of the water, caught the sun, and then, as he went back into the stream under the surface, his shadow seemed to float down the stream with the current, unresisting, to his post under the bridge where he tightened facing up into the current.

Nick's heart tightened as the trout moved. He felt all the old feeling.

—Hemingway, "Big Two-Hearted River"

AUTHOR'S NOTES

Readers may notice that the order of events in *Growing Gills* is not strictly chronological. Instead, this book follows a conceptual and thematic journey that focuses on the primary causes that I feel have made me the man that I am: family and heritage, the artistic nature of fishing, the purity of the wild, the love of fish, and the natural world as teacher. I hope that this nonlinear structure will not confuse readers, but rather will emphasize the foundations of my journey.

The chapter title "*What in me is dark, illumine...*" is an allusion to John Milton's *Paradise Lost* (1674), lines 22-23 of Book I.

Readers from Jackson County, North Carolina, may notice that the word *Tuckasegee* has been used for both river and community. *We* know the river as Tuckaseigee while the community is Tuckasegee. The publisher has decided to use the spelling found in most North Carolina atlases and gazetteers for consistency. This may indeed be more consistent, but rest assured, the two will always be a little different for us.

CONTENTS

GROWING GILLS

Growing Gills

The screen door creaked shut behind me as my girlfriend and I entered the pet store in downtown Sylva, North Carolina. Sara was immediately drawn to the puppy bins straight ahead. As she stood giddily overlooking the hounds, her petite frame, tight in jean shorts and a spaghetti strap tank top, seemed antsy. After gazing down on mixed breed mountain dogs, she looked back over her shoulder and smiled at me, but I found myself fixated on the rows of aquariums to the right. A blend of saltwater and freshwater tanks lined makeshift shelving units in the middle aisle and also ran along the back wall of the store. Colorful fish finned through bubbles in every glass box.

A pair of oscars swam in a ten-gallon aquarium on the back wall: one albino with orange and pink spots, one a tiger colored like a tabby cat. Both fish were around ten inches, nearing full growth, and sharked through the tank in search of the next meal. Oscars are aggressive fish, so as I stuck my hand over the open tank I wasn't surprised when the tabby-coated oscar exploded through the surface and bit down on the tip of my index finger. The fish sank back into the aerated water and I smiled.

I knelt down to eye level while both fish stared forward swimming to stay directly in front of me as I shifted from foot to foot. The fishes' pectoral fins rowed like paddles holding them steady. Watching their gills open and close, I felt my ears begin to move back and forth trying to mimic the motion. Buried deep in my subconscious is the memory of prenatal gills; I was created in water and a part of me has never fully dried.

I don't know where this obsession with fish stems from, but I became a fisherman as soon as my hands could grip the cork handle of a rod. By the time I was four or five, I knew how to hold a rod, set the hook, and reel. Not long after, I was obsessed.

Instead of watching cartoons on Saturday mornings, I lay tummy-down on shag carpet with my head propped on a pillow and stared at Hank Parker, Roland Martin, and Bill Dance casting lures into beds of lily pads and yanking hard into the jaws of football-bellied large-mouth bass. After the shows ended, I tied on a hook, headed to the pond, and emulated everything I had seen on television. I came home when the sun dimmed orange behind the red oaks and spent the rest of the night flip-casting barrel sinkers into a Dixie cup at the edge of my kitchen. I wanted to be a master, not for money, but for no other reason than to catch more fish. It was always about the fish, and the only way to get my hands on them was with rod and reel.

My childhood bedroom in Charlotte, North Carolina, was a temple built to worship sunfish. A forest green border with paintings of a brownish largemouth, a ragged-finned crappie, and a god-awful portrayal of a rainbow trout bordered the ceiling. A scientific chart of "Bass and Other Sunfish" with beautiful brushings of panfish and lists of Latin names hung on one wall—depictions of my own pagan gods. An oak creel lacquered to look rustic dangled from a nail just above my headboard. A large framed poster, a still-life photograph of an eclectic collection of fly-fishing gear with the words "I'm Hooked" along the bottom, was hung on the wall beside my bed. My rods stood faceted in a pine stand beside the door. Within those four walls, my life was—and is—defined.

Most nights I lay in bed and flipped through pages of Audubon field guides on fish, specifically the *North American Fishes* edition. As I learned terms like opercle, cycloid scales, and branchiostegal rays; I searched through colorful photographs for fish I'd caught, fish I'd heard about, and fish I might one day hook. I read every book, magazine, and guide I could get my hands on, determined to know everything there was to know about my scaly relatives that swam beneath the murky film.

I researched my piscine forebears as if they were the truest sense of family genealogy. I was more attached to my family with fins than I was to my own parents. Every time I watched a fish move through the water or swim from my fingertips, I felt as though I had to say goodbye to someone I loved. No matter how often I held them or saw one rise to a cricket thrusting across the surface of a pond, I never could get close enough.

I couldn't have been more than eleven when I decided I needed fish of my own. My sister, Deana, who was six years older than I, had a small, ten-gallon aquarium on her desk. I want to say that on this particular day there weren't any fish in the tank (probably a time in between toilet-destined goldfish), although I could be wrong. Whatever the case, Deana was a strawberry-blond teenager more interested in boys than pets, and I knew that her little aquarium would make a great home for new fish. Being the loving brother that I was (as well as an avid, young ichthyologist), I decided I could fix the problem of an empty tank with a few small sunfish from a local farm pond. My plan was to catch a couple of juvenile bluegills to put in the aquarium. I wouldn't keep any over four inches.

I headed to the pond with a flimsy spinning rod bobbing in one hand and a five-gallon bucket swaying in the other. The worn clay path to the pond was lined with blooming yellow jessamine, and the sweetness of honeysuckle hung on the air like perfume in the warm afternoon sun. Standing on the bank, I cast a fire orange cork into the cloudy water. Immediately I began catching fish, but that day I had to be picky: they couldn't be too big or else they wouldn't have enough room in the tank. These weren't fish fated for hot grease; these fish would be specimens for me to observe and learn from.

With three fish in the bucket, I headed home, stopping occasionally to eat fallen muscadines. I walked into the house (luckily, no one was home) and carried the five-gallon bucket, filled with scummy pond water and three fish, into my sister's room. Using a small mesh net, I scooped up each fish and placed them one by one into the tank. The first was a juvenile channel catfish about seven inches long with serrated pectoral fins and black spots covering its slate gray sides. Next, I put in a three-inch white crappie fry with specks scattered from its opaque green back down its silver body. The fish quickly descended to the colored-pebble bottom. I hadn't realized it was a crappie until I saw the elongated fanlike soft rays of its dorsal and anal fins. Then I released a young yellow sunfish about five inches long with dark moss-colored stripes running down its olive back; it swam into the bubbles and hovered near the aerator.

Granted, I had planned for a couple of small bluegills, but this was a much more scientific sample of freshwater fish; after all, now I could observe three different species at once. Unable to understand their confinement, the fish darted around quickly, ramming into the glass, but I was sure they would adapt.

Not long after putting my specimens into the aquarium, my parents and sister came home. I excitedly ran to tell them about our new pets, and they, not as ecstatic, walked into Deana's room to see.

"Lord, boy, where did you get those?" my dad asked. His forehead grew redder as he stroked his state trooper-style crew cut.

"I caught them down at the pond."

"David, you need to take them back," he urged.

"Why?"

"Well, what are you going to do with them?"

"I'm going to watch them."

"And what are you going to feed them?"

"Crickets and worms." The answers were simple to me.

"David, you need to take them back." Dad's tone was firm, but the pleas fell on deaf ears.

My parents let me keep the fish but, needless to say, nobody else in my family was thrilled about having wild fish in the house.

Just as I had planned, I caught field crickets and earthworms to feed my fish. I expected that when I dropped in the food the fish would instinctively explode on the insects, but they didn't eat. Even after all of my reading, I didn't understand that a fish could become too stressed to feed. I watched them shoot around the tank much faster than any of my sister's goldfish, as they tried to get out. Time went by and they still wouldn't eat.

After a couple of days, the water became cloudy from fish crap and decaying cricket bodies floating stiff on the surface. The smell of rotting bugs and still water was strong each time I opened the lid. I could barely see the fish anymore, and I wouldn't have even known that they were still in there if I hadn't heard them butting into glass, still unacquainted with the confines of the aquarium.

"David, you've got to do something with those fish in there. They're going to die," my mom urged. Dad had been worried about the mess, but Mom was concerned with life. She couldn't stand to watch my inadvertent torture.

"Well, what if I clean the tank?"

"You need to let those fish go. You wouldn't want them to die, would you?"

"No, ma'am."

"Then you better let them go."

"All right, I'll take them back tomorrow. It's too late to go today."

As disappointed as I was, I knew that she was right. Those fish were going to croak off, as sure as the world, and I loved fish too much to let that happen. I sat there that night, watched their silhouettes move in the hazy water, and yearned for a bigger tank; but Mom was right, and tomorrow I would let them go. Still I went to bed dreading the release.

I wish I could remember what I dreamed about that night, maybe some dream where I grew gills. What I do remember is a whole lot of yelling and hollering, loud whooping, and one angry father. I woke up to the sound of something beating against the wall that separated Deana's room from mine. Next thing I knew, my sister was screaming bloody murder (she must have thought it was a burglar). My dad ran into my sister's room, looking for an intruder to lay into. What he found was the seven-inch channel cat wedged behind Deana's desk, thrashing its head and slapping its forked caudal fin against the water-soaked sheetrock.

Pretty soon Dad walked into my room and turned on the light. I had heard all of the commotion as well as his explanation, so I knew what was going on, but I kept my eyes closed and pretended to snore. It was a Beaver Cleaver trick that never worked, but I still tried, fearing the whipping. The small catfish had burst through the surface of the water and out of the aquarium, knocking off the plastic lid and fluorescent lamp on top. Now there it lay trying to swim away on dusty carpet trapped between the desk and wall. Half-asleep, Dad did not look happy, and he had to go to work at seven the next morning.

"You need to come get this blame fish," he instructed, firm as the manager he became each day in the Pepsi plant.

"All right."

I knew he didn't want to pick the catfish up because he was afraid of getting cut by the fins, a lesson he had learned before. I walked into Deana's room where she was still sitting up in bed with blankets wrapped around her while Mom stroked her hair to calm her nerves. I wanted to laugh, but held it in as I reached behind the desk, pulled out the channel catfish, put my index and middle fingers behind the fish's pectoral blades, and held it firm with my thumb in its mouth. The catfish's thick slime enveloped my fingers, and I felt the serrated fins edging into my skin. I was too young to fear being cut. I seem to remember running over to my sister's bed to scare her with the fish and then getting yelled at, but my memory of that detail is about as foggy as the water in the aquarium.

"We need to take these fish back," Dad said.

"All right, I'll do it in the morning."

"No, David, I mean now." His voice grew more intense with each syllable.

"But Dad, it's too dark to go to the pond tonight."

"Then we'll just take them to the river. Go get the bucket."

There was nothing left to say. I got the five-gallon bucket I'd carried the fish home in, filled it with clean water from the tap, and poured the fish into it.

Dad drove me to the river in the Jeep Cherokee, stopping at River View Inn, a ragged little fish camp nestled on the banks of the Catawba River about two miles from our house. Stepping out onto the cracked asphalt parking lot, I grabbed the bucket's handle and headed toward water. A couple of Canada geese, honking in succession, were startled away from the bank as I lowered the bucket to the river. A flickering streetlight allowed me to see the three fish ride the wave of water out of the bucket as I poured the contents into the Catawba. Finally free, they swam along the clamshell-covered bottom into darkness. In the river, they were home.

In a way, I wish I could have swum away with those fish. I wish my fingers were webbed like fins and that my prenatal gills had never fully skinned over. I like to think there is a piece of my piscine past buried deep in my collective unconscious. Reading theories of recapitulation, I smile with the descriptions of ontogeny (embryonic development) mirroring phylogeny (biological evolution). I'm less interested in the connection between beginning as a single-celled organism and how I went through stages of reptilian and avian evolution; I focus on my piscine phase.

Around five weeks in human development, we have brachial arches which look like gill slits. These arches that later develop into things like the mouth, nose, neck, and larynx once carried oxygen to the rest of the body from the gills. Each arch contains a brachial pouch reminiscent of sharks' brachial clefts. During this time of development, we are cartilaginous creatures, and we have tails until shortly before we are born. I wish my gills and tail had never been absorbed back into my fetal body, allowing me to swim with the fish I feel closest to.

Although the recapitulation theory has been completely dismissed by modern science (with whom I tend to agree), I cannot ignore my connections with fishes. Something holds true in dim memories, and occasionally when I hold a trout or stare into an aquarium, this connection resurfaces. I hold onto my piscine past and throw the rest of the theory out the window because this is the only scientific answer I can find for my inherent desire to grow gills. My tail may have curled under the skin, my gills may have developed into other organs, but inside I still want to have fins and swim away.

I no longer keep fish in an aquarium, not even fish from the pet store, but my desire to observe them hasn't waned. I find it unnatural to bring fish into the terrestrial world, so instead I enter theirs. Now, when the summer sun raises the temperature of Southern Appalachian streams to seventy degrees, I swim against cool current, head submerged, watching fish dash away from my ill-attuned body. Through goggles, I gaze at schools of golden redhorses, warpaint shiners, and horny-headed river chubs shimmering through the sheen of thousands of scales reflecting sunlight like clouds of mica dust disrupted from the streambed. I see brook trout with blood red fins run through mazes of smoothed rock and disappear from sight. During these moments—I am alive.

I wish that I could tail through crevices, follow the fish into dark spaces between rocks, hide, blend into the bottom, and dart back out when the coast is clear. Instead, my 6′5″ frame wallows around like a hog in mud while the fish shoot through the stream as if water offers no resistance. The fishes' pectoral fins direct them in sharp angles like red-tail hawks' wings turning their bodies through thermals. As much as I wish otherwise, I am human. I feel closer to fish than I do my two-legged counterparts, but unfortunately I can never fully fit in underwater. Yet in moments when I see fish, my humanness vanishes and I revert.

In the shade of a fifty-foot river birch, I sit on a mattress of soft moss surrounded by trout lilies and Solomon's seal. The cold mist of a waterfall sprinkles my skin, and I see a native brook trout rise to a trico—a minute species of mayfly—laying eggs. After engulfing the mayfly, the trout vanishes among the riffles. My ears begin to move back and forth again like gills as a part of my unconscious bubbles to the surface and I feel home.

A School of Cannibalistic Fish

On the Water

Blooming mimosa trees always signaled the height of summertime bream fishing. My father first made the connection between trees and fish, but it was an event that we both came to anticipate. Dad would notice the first trees as he drove along the highways on his way home from work or to a Methodist Men's meeting. In the evening he sat in the gooseneck rocker reading the *Charlotte Observer*. His voice would come through the thin paper: "Mimosa trees are blooming." He spoke matter-of-factly, but the magnitude of each syllable hung in my ears. "Bream ought to be biting pretty good about now."

"You want to go?" I responded without looking up from the television. I was sprawled out across the worn-out sofa that had once matched the blended colors of the shag carpet. Our house was decorated in outdated 1970s furniture, fixtures, and carpeting; but the "vintage" look was not deliberate.

"Yeah, we can go this Saturday if I get the bills done in time."

My father was always an accountant, whether at home or in the office. The monotony of paperwork always came first, a routine that never made much sense to me but was just the way it was: electricity bill first, fishing second. My mind never has worked like that, a key difference between my father and me. My lights will probably be turned off sooner or later for missing a payment while I'm out on the water, but that's just a risk I'll have to take.

Dad was also a workaholic, so if he wanted to fish on Saturday, he did everything he had to do to make sure that was possible. So, late Friday night he finished the bills, and the next morning we headed for the Catawba. My mother's Jeep rattled through gears as it pulled the aluminum boat behind.

A giant mimosa bloomed along the bank of Withers Cove, the summer air intensifying the perfume of large pink flowers. Catalpa worms had spun thick nests entangling branches and leaves in shimmering threads of silk. Channel catfish and bedding bream roamed through the shallow waters beneath overhanging limbs and waited for one of the green worms to lose its grip and fall into the river. As soon as a worm touched water, the fish erupted on the helpless pupa. As the catalpas continued to fall, a late-July feeding frenzy sent triangular lines across the surface as racing pectoral fins cut Vs across the sheen: first come, first served.

Dad and I sat in faded chairs spotted by mildew, the sixteen-foot Starcraft anchored parallel to the tree line just within casting range. A muskrat swam along the bank, its wet head just above the water's surface. When the slick-haired mammal reached a fallen tree jutting out into the river along the right side of the mimosa, its head dunked under, and the muskrat was gone.

Running the point of an Aberdeen hook through the squirming rings of a night crawler, I knew the muskrat was there for the same reason we were. Dad and I weren't the only ones who knew mimosas brought schools of bream. Raccoons, muskrats, ospreys, hawks, and snapping turtles all saw the same thing each year and understood. The hairy blossoms sprouting like amaranth pink Koosh balls on the mimosa trees meant one thing: fish.

I slipped my first cast just under the tangled branches. The fluorescent orange cork skittered across the surface and came to rest in the cool shade. Within seconds the cork was high-tailing toward the fallen tree on the right. The bobber disappeared and I set the hook.

I yanked low and fast in the opposite direction of the fish, the wobbly steel rod wisping across the surface and then bowing as the tension of the sunfish set in. I wound the handle of the Quantum spinning reel, and the rod pulsated with each burst of fins. I lifted a hand-size bluegill from the river, grabbed its scaly body, ran my thumb over the spiny dorsal fin, and removed the small hook, the worm still attached but running up the monofilament line. Dad glanced over, his hazel eyes hidden behind his Ray-Ban Aviators and his red face shadowed by the brim of a desert camouflage boonie hat. He smiled and reached down, flipping the livewell switch on.

Water ran into the compartment beneath my feet as Dad made his first cast along the left side of the tree. I opened the carpeted lid of the livewell and dropped the opaque bluegill into the plastic compartment. The fish slapped against the dirty bottom as water rose in the tank. These fish were headed for hot grease. As Dad set the hook on his first catch, I knew by the end of the day we would, in the words of my Uncle Nanner, "have a whole mess o' fish."

Hot Grease

The fish that had swum in the hot current of the Catawba River were brightly colored when I caught them, but lying on the plywood board in my backyard their vibrancy had faded, the eyes had glazed over, and the gills no longer moved. Always responsible for scaling, I held the sunfishes' stiff bodies and ran the shining teeth of the scaler against the grain of their skin. The scales flicked off like specks of mica and stuck to my face, arms, and shirt. I could see white flesh beneath uplifted lines of green skin.

Dad ran the knife blade behind the pectoral fins, lopped off their heads, cut the anal vents out, and ran the knife up the stomachs, the innards seeping out like an opened bag of giblets. We threw the guts and heads into the woods for animals and took the cleaned fish inside to cook. I saw the blood smeared across the wet plywood and understood what had occurred: fish dead, nothing in vain, take only what you need, waste not, fry them hot, and eat.

On my father's side of the family eating fish was a hands-on affair. There was no need for forks or knives; we all learned to eat them off the bone. With the smell of hot grease and fried fish hanging in the air, my family would tear into fish. When I was a kid, the scene reminded me of those moments in cartoons where the cat holds the fish by the tail, shoves the fish in its mouth, and pulls it back out with nothing but the skeleton remaining.

Watching my dad and me shove catfish into our mouths, my mother's side of the family gasped and thought we would certainly get a bone caught in our throat, but in our eyes that's what the hushpuppies were for. Besides being the perfect side at a fish fry, the doughy wads of hushpuppies made sure that anything caught in the throat eventually went down. Topped off with hand-churned ice cream (a hint of rock salt sneaking into each bite from the churn), there was no better meal.

I was taught the fried fins and tails were the best part of the fish, and it didn't take much convincing for me to realize they were right. Uncle Don, my father's uncle (nicknamed "Cruiser" from late nights in pool halls), always called fried bream "potato chips." When Dad was a kid he'd walk home from Burr's Pond, and as he passed Don's house, Cruiser would yell out from his porch, "Got any tater chips?"

Crunching into the crispy tail of a bluegill, I understood why. There's no other way to describe the flavor to anyone who hasn't eaten them, and that's exactly the taste: crispy, salty, greasy, delicious. If my family knew anything at all, it was how to fish and how to eat.

We spent so many hours casting to bream and eating their fried bodies that we all started resembling the fish we caught. This may have made it hard to find suitors, but none of us minded. We were all ugly as hell but were tied close to the fish we sought. Like Vardaman's famous chapter in Faulkner's *As I Lay Dying,* "My mother is a fish," everyone on my dad's side of the family might as well have fins.

I was born into a school of cannibalistic fish. We eat our piscine brethren and always have: grilled, smoked, baked, poached, stewed, but mostly deep fried. The general rule of thumb has always been and will always be: if you can stand, you can fish. Fishing was not only a pastime for my ancestors; fish in a bucket meant one less meal that had to be bought. So, everybody in my family learned the ways of the past and the traditions continued: if you can fish, you can clean a fish, and if you can clean a fish, you can eat a fish. Early on I learned the reality of life and death by partaking in scaling the catch.

The Matriarch

I can't remember how old I was, but my family was at a Carolina beach with Granny, my father's aunt who raised him. I stood on the shore next to her as she peeled transparent shells off a couple of shrimp and threaded the curled flesh onto the two long-shank hooks of her saltwater rig. I remember my feet and legs were gritty with sand. The smell of bait was stuck in her fingernails, and her straw hat was secured to her head with a white sash. We walked to the waterline together, the long saltwater rod held firmly in the grip of Granny's age-spotted hands. I stood on the wet sand where periwinkles dug down, and I watched as she waded knee-deep into the ocean and cast the line, the pyramid sinker landing just beyond the breakers.

With the bail still open, line coming out, Granny back-stepped toward me, locked the bail, reeled in the slack, and handed the rod to me. That fiberglass rod was at least three times as tall as I, but I held tight to the worn cork grips, the butt of the rod extending to the sand behind me.

"Now, when a fish bites, it'll feel like this," Granny explained as she tapped her hand hard and fast against the brown blank of the rod.

"If it feels like this and just pulls for a minute and lets go, don't pay it no mind 'cause it's just the waves." Demonstrating the motion, she pushed down on the rod and then let it pop back up as she released her hand.

The line angled out into the ocean, and with each wave it was pulled by the breaker and snapped back up as the surge crashed ashore. The feeling of a rod being tugged on by waves is something that will make most fishermen set the hook, but Granny had shown me right. I knew the pull was not that of a fish, so I stood and waited; the gulls cawed as they held steady on the wind over the ocean, sanderlings and sandpipers scattering along the shore.

"Popper used to be able to cast way out there past them waves," Granny said, pointing toward the ocean's horizon. "Folks used to say he was fishing plumb over on the England side of the Atlantic, but he could catch some fish."

Granny spoke of her second husband, a man that I only knew through stories, a good man who died before my time. Her words were broken with clicks as she repeatedly sucked at her top teeth as if trying to get a piece of pork chop out that had been there for days. The sounds reminded me of the noises made by an angry gray squirrel, a sound that I often tried to mimic after I'd been around her. It was one of those quirks that you don't realize how much you love—or how much it defines a person—until that person's not around to do it anymore.

"Man, he could fish," she continued. "It didn't matter what we was fishing for; he'd catch them just as soon as his line hit water. Ol' Wade used to get so mad at him when we was up in the mountains fishing for trout." Wade was a friend of theirs who once tried to sell me a gun outside of church when I was in eighth grade. He was a wiry old cuss, and Granny had known him well. "Wade would be putting on all kinds of gadgets (because he was a fly fisherman, you know), and by the time he got his stuff ready, here we'd come with a stringer full of trout. Popper would tell him, 'Guess we can go on home—seeing how we done caught our limit,' and Ol' Wade would get red in the face and yell, 'Go to HELL, Popper.'"

Granny broke into a cackling laugh, and I smiled up at her as if I knew what she was talking about. I was too young to know any of the people she mentioned at that point. I've since met many of the men and women brought to life in her stories, and each was made real during my first introduction. Older now, I look back on photographs of Granny in her prime, smiling into the lens as she stands next to Popper and Wade. On the water with her, I was too young to fully appreciate what was happening. My childish mind took a tangent fairly quickly—the smell of saltwater, the swoop of a pelican, the sound of ghost crabs waltzing across the shore. I handed the rod back to Granny and turned away.

I ran back up to the lawn chairs where my parents were sitting and started playing with a bright orange bucket and shovel. Dad popped the top on a Cheerwine—that cherry-flavored soda, the staple of all my family fishing trips—and broke the silence. "She's got one."

I turned toward Granny, who was standing on the beach, and watched as she walked backwards into loose sand. The long fiberglass rod was jerking as the fish tailed through the waves. Dropping the bucket and shovel, I ran toward her and saw a gorgeous golden-colored whiting lying in the sand. It hadn't taken her long to do what I hadn't had the patience for. She picked up the fish in her tanned hands to put it in the bucket. I recall the blue veins peeping through the skin of her hands like the forks of an azure river, even her blood mimicking water. I grabbed the rod and this time I wouldn't let go.

Fish Tales

Besides being a family of fishermen, we were all storytellers. Our stories were stitched tight with details of time on the water. There was never a moment together when tales weren't swapped or laughs weren't shared. Whether we were at Thanksgiving dinner or gathered outside the church on Sundays, stories of fish caught and fish seen sprang back and forth between each other's lips, each person adding his or her own interpretation of what really happened.

I spent weekends at Granny's house rocking on a rusted bench swing, the hinges creaking with every pendulum thrust. Nestled in the crook of her arm, I listened to tales about the Catawba River but from a time when condominiums didn't line the banks and when Henry Ford was first paving toward the unknown future. Sometimes her thick southern accent rattled on about stringers of bream, jug fishing for catfish, and the fall run of puppy drum (her name for redfish) along the Outer Banks.

Granny was the greatest storyteller of us all; her stories were the root that the rest of the family's tales stemmed from. Of the stories told, some became legendary. One such tale was about a time when some of my family was flounder gigging, and one of them put a spear into something that he hadn't expected. Although I wasn't there to experience it firsthand, the details have been stamped into my memory, the spoken words setting off a scene in my mind, a scene of my own creation, but nonetheless true. The Legend of Spike is one that brings belly laughs with it, a story that seems utterly impossible, even now, until I look back at the photographs.

The Legend

Dad, Granny's son Tim, Uncle Oscar, and his son Bobby went out one night into an inlet somewhere along the North Carolina coast to gig flounder. A moonless night made the stars brighter in the summer sky as the men waded into the water in search of their prey. Each one carried a broomstick with a pronged-metal gig attached to the end, a deadly weapon against the unsuspecting flounder on the bottom.

Bobby had a rope lassoed around his waist dragging through the salty shallows a black inner tube with a plywood board underneath. A car battery rested on the wet board and provided electricity for the lights that would illuminate the outlines of flounder against the sand. Dad and Bobby held onto long sticks with light bulbs rigged to the ends, with cords running from the bulbs to the battery. The trick was to submerge the bulbs under the water before attaching the cords to the battery; otherwise, the lit bulbs would burst as soon as they touched water.

The burning bulbs provided the only focal points of light; everything else was black, nothing visible but the uneven layers of sand and shell. The inlet was only knee-deep as they waded through low tide. A wind pushing in from the east whistled across the hollow reeds and spread along both banks like waving hair. The marshlands were silent except for that low, steady, oscillating resonance of grass flutes. Blue crabs sidestepped quickly as bright light passed over their shells.

Soon enough the light exposed a flattened flounder. Only the fish's faint outline distinguished it from the bottom. Tim's dark, hairy arms gigged hard, the spear shooting through flesh and into sand. Blood slowly clouded the water around the broomstick as the flounder slapped violently against the bottom. Tim lifted the gig—water beading off the long handle, prongs driven through the starred brown flesh of the flounder—and flung the fish off the prongs into the inner tube like he was shoveling loose dirt. The flounder continued to flap against the wooden board and battery. None of them gave the fish a second glance, their eyes fastened hard on the lit sand beneath their bare feet. The fish weren't thick along the bottom but present enough that every fifteen minutes or so somebody would gig another. The inner tube was getting full with layers of camouflaged flounder lying on top of one another, and blood spilled out of the white undersides of the fishes' bodies.

As the men headed back toward their pickup truck, Bobby's light outlined another, and Uncle Oscar instinctively shot forward, the gig piercing the profile dead center. The instant prongs broke flesh, Oscar's arms went berserk as the fish jolted forward, held to the gig by pointed barbs. His shoulders rotated in figure eights like he was paddling fast in a canoe race as the fish swam in every direction in bursts of contracting muscle. They all knew that it was no flounder putting up such a fight—flounder barely bobbed the stick. Oscar, on the other hand, was being dragged through the shallows, his uneven steps sloshing through the water, the fish almost pulling him in. The battle lasted minutes for Oscar but must have seemed to go by like hours. Blood blurred the water around his wading body as he finally heaved the fish through the surface. Once it was plopped into the inner tube, they all gathered around staring down at something they had never seen before.

Back at the beach house, they cleaned the flounders on a warped board table, saved the beast for last, and walked over occasionally to stare down at the oddity in the cooler. With the flounders gutted and bagged, Oscar pulled his fish from the cooler with a pair of channel locks, scared to touch the toothy leviathan: the upturned eyes sat like marbles atop the fish's head, the gaping mouth turned upright, the giant pectoral fins like veined paddles, the olive skin freckled with white spots growing larger toward the tail. They didn't know what it was or what to do with it, so they took pictures, named it Spike, and declared it the ugliest fish in the sea. The legend was born.

Looking at the picture as Dad told the story, I stared at the details and determined, like them, that Spike was one ugly bastard, but I wanted to know exactly what he was. I searched through field guides and tried to find the answer. Finally I recognized the fish as a northern stargazer, a benthic (bottom-dwelling) species that inhabits the eastern seaboard from North Carolina to New York. They were most commonly found in water at least a hundred feet deep but could be found in sandy shallows during the spawn. Their mouths are on top of their heads so that they can suck in prey while remaining hidden on the bottom. They even have electrical organs as a defense mechanism, but I never heard of Uncle Oscar getting shocked. Their Latin name, *Astroscopus guttatus*, is a combination of two words meaning "one who aims at the stars" and "speckled," but in my family the fish has always remained Spike.

Blood and Water

I know that most families have stories of fishing trips, but with mine it's a little different. These aren't tales told and born anew each time everyone's back together. These aren't stories marking the one or two outings when a father took a son fishing. These stories are our lives, the cornerstones of our existence, the reason that we continue to wake up and give the world another go. The tales are the points along our linear journey through this world and the only thing to assure us that we ever lived. In the quilt work of our lives these are the patches stitched together by our breathing, the only thing that holds it all together. Fishing is not a hobby; it is who we are.

We are a family defined by time on the water, time shared with rods in hands. When I try to find the reason that I'm so attached to fish, it always goes back to heritage. Although my family is not the only reason to explain why I sit for hours watching trout rise to a cloud of mayflies, everything I have become (as well as my entire journey as a fisherman) can be traced back to where I came from. My roots are embedded in water like those of a cypress, and I cannot imagine it any other way.

Our chromosomes are strung with monofilament line. We are so attached to the fish we seek that it's almost as if our skin has become scaly, our limbs have turned to fins, and we swim through a world amongst people, nothing more than fish out of water. We never fit in with the crowd because unless we share blood, the crowd could never understand. We are oddities like Spike, disappearing into sand, moving only to catch a passing fish. We are bound together in the seine of the world, continuing to be drawn in closer, until another day can be shared, another legend told, another fisherman born. Every baby born into this family must hold a rod and must continue the line. I can still remember when I grew from a fry and finally joined the school.

Casting Onward

I was eleven years old when I missed a week of sixth grade in order to join my family on their yearly trip to the Outer Banks. I had never been allowed to go before, but the magic of what had occurred on Hatteras Island always gave me goose bumps, and my hairs stood on end as my father told stories after arriving home. I couldn't believe I was finally going to be a part of those tales, finally joining the ranks of my piscatorial family.

On the shore of the Atlantic, a cold November breeze blew in from the east and shifted sand along the beach. The smell of seawater was heavy on the chilling wind. Past the breakers, where the ocean calmed into one continuous straight line, the sky blended from cobalt along the horizon to a peachy orange, then into flax yellow gradually rising to white. The winter sun had sunk behind the swaying sprigs of sea oats and disappeared beneath the smoothed dunes. A slick pane of wet sand, a remnant of receding waves, shone like a sheet of ice in the dying sunlight.

My family stood along the shore, each member with a shimmering line extending from their pole into the green breakers. Darkened silhouettes grew smaller the farther the bodies stood down the beach, each shadow holding a long rod bowing to the incoming tide. The profile farthest away rotated toward the dunes as she set the hook, her rod doubling over from the tension of current and fins. Granny had a fish. Everyone along the shore turned and looked at her for a second before concentrating again on the pull of his or her own rod.

I stared at my family lining the cold shoreline, my grandmother reeling in a spot, the first stars coming into view over the ocean. We were a family of fishermen, the need for water pumping hard through each of our veins. I never had a choice about this matter, and I'm glad for that.

The rod twitched. I yanked back on the cork grip and backstepped from the shoreline into softer sand. The rod bowed to the incoming tide, and I reeled toward another tale.

Breaking In the Cork

Her hands—scattered with age spots and veins raised like roots running under thin skin, each wrinkle holding a story—stitched tight curves through the colored fabric of a Wagon Wheel quilt. Granny told me a tale about working for Union Carbide after the "last great American war," but all I could focus on as a twelve year old were her hands. Hands that had picked cotton, cleaned fish, mixed cobblers, and held young'uns now exposed brittle bones and fragile skin as delicate as tissue paper. The story of her life was spelled out across her palms, each line a narrative of her eighty years.

About that time Granny gave me one of her old spinning rods. The steel rod was chocolate brown with tan and gold thread wrapped around every guide. That rod was as flimsy as the hickory switches she used to spank my legs with and would double over every time a fish was on the line. A small Mitchell spinning reel was fastened tightly to the reel seat, but a broken screw meant to hold the arm on the reel made it impossible to cast. I dreaded taking off the old Mitchell, separating the partnership of rod and reel, but that rod begged to be fished. Saving every dime I could find, I bought a new Quantum reel and continued the tradition she had started—catching fish.

Thirteen years from the moment I first held the rod, I rocked back and forth in a tattered recliner and stared at her rod resting in the corner of my living room. The limber tip curved into convergence with the wall, the tarnished guides pressed against painted sheetrock. I walked over to the rod, eased it away from the wall, and carried it back to the chair. I sat back down, caressed the smoothed grip, and looked at every nick in the aged cork. My mind flashed back to images of her hands. The same hands that offered me cornbread had softened the layers of cork over the years.

I had held that rod many times, and I'd caught thousands of fish with it, but I couldn't take credit for such a masterpiece. The cork grip of that rod defines what it means to be a fisherman. That handle was not aged from sitting in a garage becoming a support for cobwebs or left forgotten in an attic begging to be cast. That handle was worn, smoothed, and perfected by the hands of an artisan. Holding that grip, I grasp a piece of history, continue her tradition, and, in a way, become what she was.

I don't recall her fishing with that specific rod, but my memory is chock-full of scenes of the two of us casting saltwater rigs into breakers at low tide. She held the worn grip of a 9-foot fiberglass rod and waited for the repetitive ticks of a whiting nibbling shrimp from her hooks. Her tanned arms yanked hard as she backed up the beach with her gray hair blown sideways in the wind. The cork of that rod also told stories. Sand and salt were embedded into the seams, and dried fish slime coated the cork. Buried into that grip was a piece of herself, a piece that I cherish, the fingerprints of a master.

If you ever doubt whether a man truly fishes or simply says that he does, just ask to hold his rod. It's easy to tell how consumed people are with their craft by examining their tools. Paintbrushes speckled with acrylics, shotgun barrels blued from open seasons, knife blades tarnished but sharp, cork grips worn dark and smooth—these are the signs of artisans. I can tell a lot about a man by holding the grip of his fishing rod. Unblemished handles and the cork still as tan as the freshly plucked top on a cheap bottle of wine tell the story of someone who's rarely touched water. Fish stories remain tales until I see the rod. A virgin rod will call out the lies of a so-called fisherman faster than shifty eyes give away guilty children. Cork grips are my polygraph. Show me a rod with a cork grip lacquered with fish slime, scales and sand deep in the crevices of the cork, and I'll know that person has devoted time to mastery.

An author and friend of mine, Ron Rash, had been asking me to take him fishing for years. I knew of his love for Appalachia, fly fishing, and native trout from reading his words. His descriptions are alive, so I never doubted that he had been there and that he shared my passion. The only reason I'd yet to take him on the water was because I knew he had bad knees and a stiff back. I also knew if anything happened to him while we were on the water, every bigwig at Western Carolina University would be ready to tan my hide. Through time, our friendship had grown past a master-apprentice relationship in a creative writing classroom and blossomed into a mutual respect of wild places. There was no doubt; it was time to take him fishing.

One afternoon in late spring, we met in his office and headed for a hole on the Tuckasegee River where I'd hammered fish a week before. He understood the significance of saying he was a fly fisherman to a man like me. His lyrical descriptions of native brook trout were too deliberate to be faked. I knew he probably dreamed of twenty-inch trout just as I did, and I couldn't wait to see him on the water.

Earlier that week when I'd asked Ron what he was fishing with, he had explained to me that he'd broken his bamboo rod the previous weekend. That wasn't a problem, considering I had six fly rods waiting for water, but the fact that he fished bamboo said it all: people who fish bamboo do so for one reason, tradition. Tradition comes from respect, respect from trial and error, so there was no doubt that he'd spent time waist-deep in a stream. I knew he was a fisherman.

The morning of our trip, I threw a 5-weight and a 2-weight on top of a 7-weight that had been left in the cab of my truck for night-fishing. The plan was to let him fish the 5 while I chucked dries on the limber 2-weight. When we got to the hole and parked in a red clay pull-off beside a bulldozer, I hopped out of the truck and started pulling waders over my brown Dickies, quick as a rubythroat. Ron methodically drew his Don Bailey waders onto his long legs and tightly laced his wading boots.

"There were a couple of people fishing that hole when we drove up," I told Ron. From the road, I'd seen two men in our section of river. One was on the bank gathering his gear, and the other was casting, thigh-high in the current. "What do you want to do?"

"Well, we could kill them." He spoke with a thick Appalachian accent. There was seriousness in his voice like a character from a Faulkner story.

"With luck, they'll be gone by the time that we get down there," I said. The water would have already been touched, but I hoped that the fishermen hadn't pressured the trout too hard.

"We could kill them," he repeated with little expression. "There are plenty of places to hide the bodies." High in Appalachia, I knew he was right. The mountains held plenty of places to dump a body or two where no one would stumble upon the remains. Continuing the scenario, I thought to myself that we were there to fish, and a messy cleanup would mean less time on the water.

Ron was tall and lanky like myself. He'd run track in college, and the thirty or so years since hadn't changed his thin frame. Brownish gray hair parted across his head, and the scruffy, unshaved stubble on his face held the same color. His steel blue eyes reminded me of the way a hound's are set, with a certain seriousness and sadness in their stare. Ron's hands looked like they'd spent time doing work, scratching stories, and holding rods. I would have liked to have seen his broken bamboo rod, to hold the grip, and to understand how it had been fished; but today he would add a few lines to my cork and that was fine by me.

I grabbed the olive rod tube out of the cab and unzipped the cover, unveiling my baby: a gorgeous 5-weight rod with the cork grip aged to perfection in my hands and a tarnished reel held firm against the rosewood seat. I tried to unscrew the reel from the rod so that Ron could put his onto it. I would have preferred his just using my reel, but he's left-handed, making my line and drag setup backwards in his hands. "Now, Ron, you know this reel ain't ever come off this rod," I said, half-jokingly as I struggled to loosen the reel away from the reel seat.

"Is that right?"

"Yeah, I think it's bad juju to take a reel off a rod." I was kind of kidding with him, but the strain of getting the reel off made me wonder. I see the relationship between reel and rod as a marriage that never needs a divorce. If something breaks on the reel, I'd rather retire the whole outfit than separate the two. The retaining ring finally broke free and the reel fell into my palm. I handed the 8½-foot rod to Ron and began putting the sections of my 2-weight together. He tightened the rings on a battered Medalist reel he'd had since childhood.

We were both pulling our leaders and line through the guides when I heard something really strange—under his breath, Ron had cursed. The reverberation of that single syllable echoed through my eardrums. It wasn't that the word bothered me; I had just never heard this man who commands language revert to the archaic utterances I was so accustomed to using. I looked up from the tippet I was fastening to my leader, and Ron stared, puzzled, tender-eyed as a beaten dog. In one hand he held my rod, and in the other hand, the top section from between the last guide and the tip-top.

"I broke your rod." He spoke as if someone had died.

"Ah, it's all right." I forced each word from my lips. My heart sat low on my stomach like a fat man sinking into the cushions of a worn-out couch. I wasn't mad, not even frustrated, but I was dumbfounded. I stood in horror but sucked it up and didn't let any emotion show. Ron was too good a friend, and I respected him too much to let a fumble ruin our day on the water.

"I don't know what happened. I was just pulling the leader through the guides and it snapped. It wasn't like I was pressing real hard on it." He repeated his motion with his hands. "I don't know what happened."

To this day I don't think that Ron did anything to break that rod. I think that there was a weak spot in the graphite, probably a result of something I had done, but he felt awful. "Don't worry about it. I'll just let you use this 2-weight, and I'll fish with the 7-weight I've got in the truck."

"Now, David, I ain't going to let you take me fishing unless you let me buy you another one just like it." He meant every word; I could read it in his stare.

There was no arguing. I'd have to let him buy the rod. "Fine. You fish this 2-weight and I'll fish my other rod. Don't worry about it."

Bad luck continued when I lost my truck keys, but I was unfazed, knowing that I was about to be wrapped in the cool embrace of a trout stream. I don't know for sure that Ron shared the same attitude, but for me it was easy. Screw it, I thought, at least I'm going fishing.

On the stream, trout were feeding fairly consistently. The fish weren't coming to the surface, but I could see their shadowy bodies ascend to take drifting nymphs. I was sure we were going to get into some fish, and judging from the luck I'd had there the previous week, I thought one of us might have a shot at a monster.

My assumptions about Ron being a fisherman were right. His overhead cast was nice, but when he cast side-armed, he was an artist.

His side-arms swept line under low oak branches overhanging the bank, his mends were marvelous, and his instinctive ability to read water was the final answer. One thing I wasn't right about, however, was that we would catch fish.

Two hours on the stream and neither of us had gotten a bite. Finally, I hooked one small, stocked brookie, but besides that we were skunked. The fish I caught is hardly worth mentioning, but I've got to try to find one bright spot. Ron got a decent bite, but by the time he raised the rod, the fish was gone. His hand was quick on the draw, but the fish was a runner, rising and disappearing in an instant, what pheasant hunters would call a cock that flushed wild.

With the April sun slowly vanishing behind the ridge, we headed to the truck with our tails between our legs. The fish were there, but they wanted nothing to do with our feathered hooks. Trout:1 – Us:0. We left it at that.

On the way back, I found my truck keys stashed in the back of my vest. We said our goodbyes, tried to come up with a decent excuse, and vowed to fish again. Then, as if things couldn't get any worse, Ron drove off toward his home in Clemson, a solid hour and a half away, with my reels safely in his trunk. When I hadn't been able to find my keys, I had stashed my valuables (a Fly Logic 2-weight reel and a Ross size 7) in his trunk. By the time I realized it, his car was winding around curves toward South Carolina. One of us (and I don't know which), or maybe both, was karma's bitch for the day.

Driving home, I began thinking about that broken rod. I hadn't let it show when Ron was around, but I was devastated, heartbroken, depressed. When I had time to think about what had happened, I felt sick, close to vomiting. I thought about that rod, broken and unfishable. It wasn't so much the rod in its entirety, but the cork grip that I held so close. That cork, originally manila-colored and dusty from sanding, had been worn to a beautiful brownish green. It had been smoothed to a slick and shiny finish. More than that, my hands had held that grip when I reeled in the biggest trout of my life. It was more than a grip; it had become an extension of my hands and a symbol of my devotion to fly fishing. I hadn't told Ron, but that model rod had been discontinued, and there was no way I'd find another one. That rod would never fight a fish again.

Ron emailed me shortly after that trip to let me know he had my reels. I don't remember exactly what he wrote, but he jokingly said there was no way I'd take him fishing again. Despite our previous bad luck, we went again, and on that trip Ron, his son, and I all caught native brookies out of a tiny mountain creek. The fish were gorgeous, but more importantly we enjoyed seeing each other in our element. Bad days come with the territory, but we are, after all, fishermen.

Some folks are into buying the nicest rod on the market. They'll spend thousands of dollars on a Hardy, Scott, or Sage, all the time believing that the most expensive equipment will make you a fisherman. As for me, I want a rod worn with age, a rod that has seen water, a rod that has held strong while bowing to the weight of fish, and the cork grip better be right.

I'm addicted to rods. I find them in yard sales, on eBay, or in antique stores. I see them tilted against a back wall like Granny's, begging to be fished. Something in me can't resist and I buy them. I don't have a use for all of them, but I can't stand to see the legacy of a fisherman waste away amidst cobwebs and dust. I imagine those rods being given to some unappreciative family member after the owner has died. I imagine the inheritor having no understanding of what that rod means, being blind to the stories hidden in the cracks of the grip. When I see these rods, I know, and I will not let them die. Those bought fishermen can have their thousand-dollar rods. They can believe that expensive equipment will catch them more fish or, if nothing else, make them look like they know what they're doing. As for me, give me a handle with teeth marks embedded from when I climbed a waterfall without a hand to spare. Give me a cork grip with mica pushed deep in the crevices from the times I laid the rod on the ground to admire a native brookie. I want a rod that changes just as I do, the cork slowly molded into hand, finally fitting perfectly, as man and grip fuse in partnership. The cork holds the imprint of hands, imprints only left by time spent casting, imprints that define the time invested by an artisan, and they are beautiful.

The Piscatorial Picasso

On hands and knees I crawl stealthily across rocks worn round. I snake my way to the next hole, dissect every inch of water, and constantly question, "Should I come from the right or left? Am I going to spook the guard fish if I take another step? Where is the prime feeding position? Will the alpha trout be lying there—or maybe there?" It's a game of becoming animalistic. I revert to my reptilian psyche and contemplate only the necessary. These moments rarely come and then dissolve quickly, but during those brief glimpses, I transcend humanness and become one of them. We humans are still animals; it's just that most of us have forgotten, redefining the human experience and slowly destroying the innate instincts that once made us who we were.

When I become wild, I am no longer a fisherman in the general sense of the word. At these times of complete connectedness, I am to trout as bears are to salmon; I am to fish as ospreys are to herring. My senses take over: perfect cast, hold it there, mend the line, invisible tension, wait, strike, hook set, fish. When it all goes perfectly, the fly is no longer simply chicken feathers tied to a piece of chemically sharpened metal. The fly becomes a caddis, a stonefly, a mayfly, a beetle, a bug caught in the current—completely helpless, fish food. There is no evidence that I am there. The fish do what they do, and I exploit their vulnerabilities. Predatory, I use brains rather than claws or teeth to catch trout, but the instinct is the same.

True fly fishing is not dumb fishing. There is no chucking worms and waiting. There is no cooler sitting, beer drinking (at least not during), hooks in drunken fingers. This is an art, an art that I may never fully master, an animalistic medium, one that, unless experienced, cannot be understood. Yet, if people are privileged enough to witness it, they'll know they are in the midst of a piscatorial Picasso. I've seen it; a few times I've been part of it; but every time I was there I was enamored, ensconced in timelessness.

When I see a trout rise to a fly or turn on a nymph, pressure builds in my chest nearing explosion. This is when the artist knows to wait: oftentimes I do, but at other times the urge becomes too much, always resulting in a missed fish. When I'm patient, I raise my rod tip at just the right moment, feel the tension, and play the fish, always careful not to play them too long (extended fights build lactic acid resulting in death), but just enough to let the smile creep up my shaggy cheeks. I wet my hand in the cold current to avoid removing the fish's slimy coat, remove the hook, marvel in the piscine beauty, kiss the trout on the nose, and release it.

I never drop a fish into the water; this completely ruins the experience. Holding a trout loosely in my hand, I lower the fish under the surface and face it into the current, forcing oxygen through the gills, thereby allowing the trout to catch its breath. Fully recovered, the fish fins away, sinks into the pebbly bottom, and disappears among the riffles. After the release, I sit there, smoke a cigarette, and wish that I could stay there forever, euphoria never dissipating. Then the uncontrollable desire rekindles, and soon I'm off to the next fish.

Through my evolution as a fisherman, I've come to respect certain species more than others. I don't know why exactly, but certain fish are higher on the totem than others. More so, some fish transcend all other species and deserve their own totemic monument. These fish are trout. I'll never intentionally kill a trout. Plenty of other fish (catfish, bream, crappie, croaker, whiting, spots, pompano) I'll catch, kill, and cook with regularity, but I could never inflict that same fate upon a trout. A wild trout swimming in untainted water is so perfect that I regret disturbing the scene, much less taking from it. Holding a native brookie, watching its mouth rhythmically open and close in the current, I am completely aloof from the human experience.

The green marbled back, burning red spots scattered like glowing embers, golden stomach, and fire orange pectoral fins tipped with white of a spawning brook trout cannot be fully captured by words. I have never seen colors so magnificent. Not to say the coloration of other trout is not equally astonishing, but the brooks are the only trout native to Appalachia (kindred to my own Carolinian blood), so we have something in common. Trout are the most well-dressed fish in the world, and the brook trout is the Armani of them all.

I didn't start off catching trout. In fact, I had never caught a trout—besides seatrout—until I was nineteen years old. As with most freshwater fishermen, I began my journey casting light spinning tackle for sunfish, bass, and catfish in farm ponds and rivers. Freshwater trout remained a mythic creature that swam in cold mountain brooks and were wary of any angler's offering.

Around the age of twelve, I made the progression to fly fishing. This decision came as a natural stage in my angling development. I was merely an artist in search of his medium. I didn't know the technicalities of the sport (often using straight monofilament as a leader and tippet), but there was something poetic about throwing tight loops from bank to bank. I had no one around to teach me the techniques, so I spent a lot of time hung up in the oaks and hickories, eventually learning most of the methods out of necessity rather than from teachers. As Emerson wrote, "We thrive by casualties."

I can still remember the first fish that I ever caught on the fly. Fishing what I had dubbed a "Bumblebee" (actually a McGinty), I cast into the middle of Johnston Pond, and let the fly slowly sink into the clouded water. Suddenly the fluorescent orange floating line leapt forward. I had no clue how to set the hook; I just started reeling. Luckily, the juvenile bluegill hooked itself and, after a short retrieve, I held the feisty sunfish in my hand. Its dark blue sides like a late evening sky faded into blackish orange around the belly. My fly held firm in the side of its jaw. I let the fish swim, but I was hooked. I've spent the last thirteen years trying to perfect my art, fly rod practically glued in hand, cork grips worn bare.

I still use spinning equipment occasionally to entice certain fish (I've crossed bridges, but never burned them), but I refuse to catch trout on a spinning rod. Bait fishing or any other type of spin fishing is sinful in regards to trout, blasphemous to a fish so divine. These fish are too aesthetically beautiful to be caught in such a barbaric, bungling way. Trout are pieces of natural artwork, like glowing auroras or changing leaves, and the only medium deserving of such beauty is a fly rod.

I came to this conclusion after the first time I caught wild trout on the fly. A friend of mine, Zac, one of the few true artisans that I've ever fished with, opened my eyes. A tall, slender-framed highlander, Zac was born and raised in the hills of Burke County, and his roots were evident in his thick Appalachian voice. Watching his long arms shoot bow-and-arrow casts under overhanging rhododendron, throw upstream mends to keep the fly steady in shifting currents, and sweep hook sets just below branches is breathtaking. Showing me the ways of trout, he took me up a tributary of Caney Fork Creek named Piney Mountain Creek, in North Carolina's Southern Appalachians.

On that creek, he taught me to read water like words from a page, scan currents like poetry, and dissect pools like Faulkner novels.

Wading through the cool ripples, I was completely aware that I had never entered a place so wild. Aside from the abandoned, overgrown logging road, there was absolutely no sign of human passage. Pines towered from the peaks, rhododendron blanketed the hillside, foliage shattered the sunlight, and the tiny creek ran through it all. I instantly started searching the water for likely spots, planning to use my lifetime of pond knowledge on wild trout.

"Cast right there," Zac said. "There'll be a fish there." His 8-foot rod pointed at a small pocket at the edge of a plunge pool. I thought that he was out of his mind. I didn't see any way that a fish would be holding in that sliver of water. Still, I dappled a cast into the clear, swirling eddy, keeping the line taut, rod raised high. Within seconds, the size 14 Stimulator was sucked under. The rod tip pulsated as the native brook trout used the current for heightened propulsion. I lifted the fish to the surface as the brookie tried to dig back to the unseen. Dipping my hand into the stream, I brought the fish into my palm.

I held the small brookie in my hand, its head extending from my loose fist, and removed the hook from the fish's mouth. I released my grip, palming the trout's fleshy, tender body, and witnessed all of the magnificence of its beauty: eyes like copper coins with shimmering black pupils, deep sunset orange lining the bottom of the fish's gill slits and covering the featherlike pectoral fins, goldenrod yellow visually erupting along the fattened belly. The sea green color of its back with darker pine-colored segments ran through like veins in marble, and the blood red spots dotted the trout's sides like shimmering planets.

Struck by its splendor, I held the brookie almost too long, but snapped from my trance and let the eight-inch native shoot from my fingertips back into the masking sheen. I was in love.

That first native fish is seared deep into my memory more vividly than any other experience; it plays back like a movie I can't help rewinding and watching again. We caught fish the rest of that day, all beauties, but nothing comparable to the excitement of that first encounter. From that day forth, for me, there has been no other way to catch a trout.

Since that first native trout, I've spent thousands of hours on the water in search of those fish. I've traded my elementary Johnston Pond education for a doctorate in trout water. The fish that were once mythical have become so real that I can smell their sweet, earthy aroma emanating from my hands, even on days that I've not touched water. I am haunted by their existence and by knowing they are holding steady in the current just out of sight, waiting for a meal to be brought into their feeding line. When I am left to my own thoughts, nothing else swims through my mind but trout and ways to catch them. I daydream of drag-free drifts over rising trout and of watching the slow methodic ascent of a feeding fish.

I haven't found any other fish comparable to trout: brown trout with pitch black spots covering the colors blending down their bodies from raw umber to a buttery yellow like the top of a perfectly baked biscuit; rainbows with rosy cheeks, moss green backs, cherry red lateral lines, and black specks sprinkled like pepper; and the brookies resembling marble slabs delicately brushed and speckled with brilliant yellows, oranges, and reds. These fish are masterpieces of the natural world, paintings that do not need another stroke. Every encounter is an art show; the stream is my Louvre.

Yet, the only way to experience this artwork is to catch a trout. In some crazy way, when I fish I feel involved in the process of creation. Without my participation, I would never see the beauty in its entirety, only brief flashes of color beneath the mirror of water as fish turn, one-second glimpses as trout burst through the surface and engulf emerging mayflies, or short-lived glances of red fins spooked upstream. Throwing silent loops across the surface and laying the fly delicately over holding fish, I bring what is unseen to light.

The water remains humbling. As soon as I think I've finally found all the answers, I walk away dumbfounded by the mystery of the unattainable. Fly fishing is a medium that never can be fully mastered, just as the greatest artists will never grasp every technique. Hoping for the unfeasible, the final masterpiece, keeps me committed.

I dream of a twenty-inch native brook, hooked mouth rimmed in red and gaping. Russet brown eyes, broad emerald back, red and yellow spots lustrous as jewels, flaming orange stomach with fins lined in white—it will all be there. I will devote a lifetime to mastery. This fish will be my magnum opus, my reason to cast. With the sun fading purple behind hemlock peaks, I brush curving strokes of fly line across the velvet May sky in hopes that the trout will rise. When the fish remains a ghost, I take a deep breath, lift my rod, and cast again—just one more stroke toward perfection.

Throwing Tight Loops

I sat on a large mat of moss under branches of overhanging laurel as Zac made his approach in Piney Mountain Creek. The pool he'd noticed probably held a trout, but most fishermen would not have given it a second glance due to its location. The birdbath-size pool gathered along the opposite bank beneath a thick tangle of rhododendron branches.

Thick cover and tiny pockets was a standard scenario in the North Carolina high country. Anyone who'd been there knew that traditional overhead, sidearm, and roll casts were out of the question. These types of casts would certainly lasso the tippet and fly around limbs like Indiana Jones's whip. A bow-and-arrow cast might get the fly in but keeping the offering steady would still be impossible. If it had been my lead, I would have kept tromping upstream, but not Zac. He was different.

Zac was tall and lanky, much like me, and strangers often asked if we were brothers when we ordered a round of beers, shot pool, or ate coarse-chopped barbeque at Dillsboro Smokehouse. His hair was lighter than my dark brown stubble, but through the haze of mountain fog we probably looked pretty damn close. The biggest difference was clear to me: he handled a fly rod like I dreamed of doing. Sometimes I think Zac must have been born with a fly rod in his hand.

Zac held the cork grip of the 5-weight Sage in his teeth as he slowly crawled toward the overhang, careful not to spook any fish.

Water pushed around the patched knees of his waders, and his hands gripped the slick stones covering the creek bed. A large, flat piece of limestone forced water to the far side, the barrier creating the current of the pool.

He sneaked onto the smooth boulder, sat up on his knees, detached the dark, size 12 Hendrickson from the hook keeper, and pulled just enough line from the spool to give him some play. Tugging on the bend of the dry fly, he began to bow his rod, the added tension creating a load of potential energy. He bent down, took aim, and fired the fly just beneath the spearhead-shaped leaves of rhododendron. Then he balanced one hand on the rock as the dry fly landed calmly in the center of the pool.

Zac bent down further to watch and began flicking upstream mends to keep the fly steady, the 8-foot rod reaching beneath the limbs. I'd never questioned whether or not he could shoot a cast into the tiny pocket, but I did wonder how he'd manage to hold the fly there long enough to tempt a trout. As he rolled continuous curves through the line and leader, it became clear that he knew exactly what he was doing.

A fish slapped the surface in the shady flow of water, Zac ripped the rod back across his chest, and the trout was hooked. What had seemed impossible at first became a reality as he pulled the stout native beneath the tangled limbs. I had no doubt that I was in the presence of greatness.

In fly fishing, there are few things more important than the cast. With trout being as jittery as a backwoods moonshiner crossing state borders, the delicacy of a fisherman's presentation makes or breaks an opportunity. If the fly lands too hard, the impact will unnerve the fish. If the line comes too close, the fish will jet upstream. If the shadow of the fisherman, rod, or cast becomes visible, the trout will disappear beneath stone ledges. The fact is, the cast is most often the difference between fish and no fish, and mastering a technique for every situation is an art form.

In other forms of fishing, pros master similar techniques. Bass fishermen learn to flip, pitch, swing, and skip lures into tight corners where largemouths hide. Truth be told, if you want to catch fish, then you have to be able to cast into hairy spots. If somebody tells you they've never thrown into trees, snagged stumps, or bounced lures across docks, then the odds are they aren't casting.

In high school, I used to fish with a buddy named Grady who was born, raised, and lived in a cove of the Catawba River. Some mornings I'd pile rods and tackle into my mother's minivan and then, once at school, I would put them into the bed of Grady's Z-71 pickup. When the dismissal bell rang, we would race to his truck, hop in, I'd pack a dip of snuff, he'd take a wad of chaw, and we'd head toward the river.

On the way we usually discussed where we would go, what we'd fish with, and how many we'd catch. With the whizzing of a buzzbait Grady held out the window of the speeding Chevy (he said it made the lure spin better on the water) and the smell of Redman chewing tobacco in the cab, we'd head back to his river house and jump in the sixteen-foot Boston Whaler.

For the rest of the day (and often into the night), we'd cover lots of water in an attempt to catch bass. After sunset, he'd motor up the river to River View Inn where my mom would meet us at the dock. We caught hundreds of fish together on that river, but Grady's one memorable cast separates him from other people with whom I've spent time on the water—a cast that made him an artist.

We'd spent that afternoon pinpointing big bass that were holding on spawning beds in the heat of early summer. When we found them, we offered white or chartreuse floating worms and shad-colored slug baits to the aggressive fish guarding the fry. It didn't take much. If the bait came anywhere near the sandy bed where the fish held, the bass exploded on sight. The largemouths were in the heyday of the spawn, and anything that came close was a threat. In other words, we were casting to a group of overprotective mamas and papas.

Grady and I had caught our fair share of fish that day, but as we trolled around the final cove we both continued to scan for beds. Peachleaf willows and river birches stretched out over the water. A single house was planted in the cove, and the owners had constructed a sand beach for lying out beside a covered dock. I spotted a dark circle beneath the floating pontoon boat tied off to their dock. I pointed to the spot beneath the boat, and Grady saw the bed fifteen feet back from the edge of the pontoon's outboard. It was definitely a bass bed, but I certainly didn't have a cast in my repertoire that could land the worm under that floating pontoon.

"Wish I could ease a cast back in there," I muttered to Grady, my words sloshing as the Copenhagen juice came onto my tongue.

"I can get it back there," Grady claimed, before spitting chew off the side of the Boston Whaler, a string of brown saliva running down his chin. His country accent was full of pride as he scratched his bare back, the smell of suntan oil floating to the rear of the boat.

"How you going to manage to do that?" I asked.

"Skip cast."

"What the hell's a skip cast?"

"Well, hold on a minute and I'll show you." The spit still stuck to his chin and dried in the May sun. A pale tan line (from where his glasses usually sat) ran around his green eyes and back into his blonde hair.

Grady maneuvered the trolling motor, directing the boat toward the dock, and we slowly drifted along in front of the pontoon. With a long spinning rod in his hand, he swung the rod low across the water, his arm sweeping parallel to the surface. The chartreuse worm hit water about one foot back beneath the edge of the pontoon and then began skipping farther like a well-thrown river stone. The skips came close together as the lure went out, finally skittering to a stop a few feet past the bed. I was in awe.

With a few jerks, Grady wagged the worm across the surface and as it moved above the darkened circle of sediment, a bass erupted on the bait. He pulled the fish away from the dock pilings and managed to ease the bass from beneath the pontoon boat, his rod pushed into the water to keep pressure.

After a short battle, Grady pulled the six-pound largemouth into the boat. The fish's fattened belly was full of eggs, and the dark green lateral line separated olive from white on the bass's flanks. Grady's fist fit easily into the fish's mouth to retrieve the swallowed lure. He stood there smiling proudly, his hand clutching the giant bottom lip, the massive gill plate protruding along the back of his hand.

I was stunned by how effortlessly Grady had skipped the worm under that boat. The cast would have been impossible for me to make at the time, but he shot the lure into the watery realm without thinking twice. It was the cast, not the amazing catch that mattered. It wasn't like Grady had invented the cast (he'd probably picked it up from his Bass Pro neighbor who was on "the tour"), but the fact that he could use it so effectively inspired me. Having tricks up your sleeve for the right situation separates the average fisherman from the master, and in that sense Grady was an artist on the water.

Some fishermen see casting as a competitive sport where the winner is the one who can chuck his rig the farthest. I always got a kick out of listening to Granny tell stories about her husband Popper casting "plumb across the ocean," but I knew casting was not all about distance. Sure, there are times when hurling shrimp a bit farther past the breakers or spey casting a few feet longer to running steelhead might catch more fish. Generally speaking, a fisherman's ability to get a cast into the right spot, at the right moment, and to keep it there, earns him the strike.

I've read about fly-casting competitions, consisting of different types of challenges from accuracy to distance, where winners might cast a fly more than a hundred feet. All I could think was why? Sure, it's amazing that a person can heave a weight forward line a hundred feet when I can only manage to shoot out sixty or seventy before the line becomes a limp noodle, but I've never once encountered a situation on the water where a hundred-foot cast would have gotten me a bite.

These competitions would make more sense on the stream, in real situations, where yardsticks don't matter, and with competitors facing on-the-water scenarios such as these: There are crosscurrents everywhere, and one tiny pocket of still water is holding a fish; keep the fly steady for twenty seconds. You're in a tunnel of thick cover, and one tiny hole in the laurel is your only chance to hit the seam; make the cast.

To me this would be the way to separate strong-armed yuppies from true artists. There's plenty of talent and rhythm involved in making that hundred-foot cast, but true artisans are made on the water. They are made in places where smart approaches—and a skill-set of twenty-foot presentations—are the difference between taut and loose lines. Fishermen with a cast for any situation are rare, with most folks still throwing lasso loops toward stocked trout. The ones that do exist are artisans, and most of the time I'm envious.

A few years ago, I set off during the peak of fall to tempt spawning trout to take my flies. The water on the Tuckasegee River was low, exposing a long stretch of the stone bottom, the rocks colored tan with dried clay. I walked along the dried rocks, the fires of fall burning on every hillside, and made my way upstream toward the section where water unsettled into ripples.

I began the motion of throwing tight loops of floating line toward the head of the pool. As the final curl rolled out across the surface and the fly made its way toward the head, I twitched my wrist back, sending one last curl toward the Kaufman's Stonefly, tucking the imitation under the remaining line at the last second. The tuck cast was a trick I'd learned in a Joe Humphreys essay on nymph fishing; it was one he'd learned from George Harvey to allow the nymph time to get down deep before the line, caught in the current, brought the weighted fly toward the surface.

The stonefly sank and I began throwing upstream mends to keep the fly moving naturally through the run. The mends kept the racing line from speeding up the drift as the stonefly bounced along the freestone bottom. I watched for sudden twitches in the leader, a slight stop by the line or an invisible bump by a sluggish trout. I played it perfectly, textbook nymphing with a slow natural drift, but a trout never took.

As the stonefly edged toward the end of the run, I lifted the rod with the line coming toward me and then going slack, and roll cast back toward the head of the pool. The cast unfolded across the water, droplets spraying from the lifting line, and the fly dropped quietly beneath the stirring ripples. Then the process began again: upstream mends, keep the line off the water, rod high, watch for takes, lift, roll cast. Over and over, I tried to tempt the trout that I knew was there. Nothing bit, but nonetheless I was satisfied.

I was satisfied because of the cast, because of the ability to keep my fly doing exactly what I wanted beneath the surface, because the stonefly danced calypso along the bottom, because I had made it do so. A smile sank deep on my face as I headed upstream, and despite the fact my hands lacked the sweet perfume of held trout, I was happy.

The sun's last rays made the mountains look like exploding fireworks as the yellows, oranges, and reds blended into one continuous flame. I'd caught a few trout as the day progressed, but now I stood sweeping a Prince Nymph beneath the bows of a red maple in its prime. The line just missed the leaves and limbs as the cast curled across the river. The Prince dropped into the current along the cut bank, and I fished the run out beneath the tree.

I had few fish to speak of that day (and now I can't even remember what I caught), but what remains vivid are the casts. My line wrote cursive in the sky, solidified my boundaries, and confirmed the existence of open spaces. In a way, those casts made everything else real by making me focus on the barriers. I stared at trees because the cast had to miss them. I read the current because I had to sustain the drift. I saw the sunset because my eyes focused on the tail of my backcast.

For once, I'd played every scenario perfectly, a rare event in my life as a fly fisherman. I encountered obstacles and drew correctly from my bag of casts to get the fly to the fish. No situation arose that

I didn't have an answer for. I experienced one of those short-lived moments when I too became an artist on the water. Now, when I'm untangling my fly from flexible dogwood limbs, I try to dismiss the frustration, remember days like that one, and know that the cast is there. When I find it, oftentimes the trout, the brutal critic of my art, will rise to the offering.

Feed 'em Feathers

Bellied up to a dorm room desk covered in ratty wood-grain laminate, I first learned to tie flies on a Renzetti Presentation, a vise far too fine for my fumbling fingers. Zac had invited me to sip cold beer and watch him tie a couple of patterns. Being the fishing nut that I am, I jumped at the opportunity to learn the art of fly tying. Creating a fly that would bring a finicky trout off the sandy bottom of a mountain creek seemed mystical to me. I was determined to learn so I could experience what it was like to fool a fish with my own design.

Zac opened the solid oak door, and we walked into his hot dorm room at Western Carolina University. The smell of settled weed smoke and stew beef simmering in a crockpot filled the room. Poor circulation made the air thick and sticky, and sweat immediately beaded on my forehead as I entered. Zac walked around the bed, which had books piled high on the rumpled comforter and sheets draping onto the floor, and pulled up the aluminum-framed window. He propped a box fan outward between the windowsill and window to suck the air from the room. I moved the books off the edge of the bed and took a seat on the mattress.

Zac's Burke County blood had toughened him into a man; evidence lay in the thick scar running down his throat from a knife fight. His bony fingers, slender as my own, reached for a half-smoked blunt roach that had been mashed out on the windowsill. He lit the spliff, sat back in his chair, and reached for a banjo propped on a stand in a corner of the room. Zac exhaled clouds of yellow smoke, which were instantly sucked from the room by the fan. He strummed resonating twangs on the tight strings of the banjo.

"You know my daddy played a gig on *Hee Haw* long time ago," Zac muttered. The syllables were pushed through a nearly closed mouth as the burning roach dangled from his lips, his head tilted back to keep smoke out of his eyes.

"Huh?"

"I swear to you. He knew Lester Flatt and Earl Scruggs. Hell, he's still building banjos. Says he's gonna make me one for graduation."

"Really?"

"Yeah. I got him on tape, if you want to hear him."

I nodded.

"You want a beer?" Zac put the roach out on the windowsill, blew out the last bit of smoke, and headed toward the kitchen. Zac was a good bit older than I and lived in a married dorm that was equipped with mediocre kitchens, something we single students weren't lucky enough to have. He lifted the glass lid off the crockpot, and moisture rolled down the sweaty glass and back into the broth and hot steam bellowed out. He plopped the lid back on, side-stepped to the fridge, and pulled out a German-style growler full of a coffee-colored stout brewed in downtown Sylva by a local man named Dieter. Zac unlatched the top of the container, grabbed a blue-tinted glass from the counter, and poured me a beer. The thick stout, named Black Forest by the German brewer, sat heavy in the faceted glass, a nice caramel-colored head foaming atop thc beer.

"I don't ever like to tie flies till I get my head right," Zac said, nodding to ask my agreement as he handed me the glass of beer.

"I got you. Ain't nothing wrong with a little inspiration."

I had stopped smoking pot a year prior, forced by an overload of hallucinogens, but I had no problem partaking in a full-bodied brew.

I turned up the glass and took a long hard swig of the cool mountain beer. It tasted slightly like coffee but was thick as syrup. Zac headed toward a little nook, a segue between the main room and bathroom. "Come on in here and let's tie a couple," Zac called from the nook.

Tying flies is an art form that takes the fisherman one step closer to the fish he seeks. Most fishermen simply buy flies, dig worms, or chuck molded plastic plugs; but the fly tier has the opportunity to create something that will truly fool the fish. More than that, the ability to create an artistic rendering of a mayfly spinner that can be cast into the morning fog creates a connection to place unfelt by most anglers. Besides the flies, the materials used attach the fly tier to the natural world. Walk into any fly shop, sort through the rows of hanging materials, and there will be no way to deny the inherent beauty of the wild. While animal rights activists may tremble at the sight of tanned chickens, rabbits, turkeys, pheasants, squirrels, and jungle cocks, I've gained a respect for animals that I could never get that close to otherwise.

My appreciation for animals' beauty has only increased by staring into the tanned hides of the birds and small mammals I use for fly tying. I've found details in their skins that I never would have noticed: the iridescent bars on the tan feathers of a pheasant's breast, the thick underfur holding tight to the skin beneath the coarse hairs along an elk's flank, the shifting colors of peacock plumage turning shades like black opal, the long guard hairs shooting from the cheeks of a hare's mask. Details become much more vivid when they are close enough to touch.

Yet, I understand the danger of using animals for my own private practice. The yellow flicker, a small species of woodpecker that used to flourish in the Southern Appalachians, was hunted to endangerment by fly tiers who wanted their spiny yellow feathers to tie an effective pattern known as the Yaller Hammer. I've read of cocks being bred specifically for longer, fuller cape feathers, just so fly tiers can get more flies from a single bird. Again, I'm caught as I wonder about the human impact on the wild. What right do we have to muck with nature just for our own selfish pleasure?

Still, the more I tie, the more my world is shaped by the art. I watched and studied the body structure and habits of velvet ants as they stood up like dragsters and quickly scattered along red clay beneath bent blades of grass. I've read books about stream entomology and emergence patterns of insects. I stare at the way a caddisfly's wings are wet down as the bug steers too close to water, is sucked into the current, and floats by while I wade through the river.

On the other hand, I see products in drugstores and think, "Damn, that looks like the tail of a trico," or "Man, that's just like the segmented body of a stonefly." I've used fake fingernails to mimic the hard abdominal shells of beetles, I've tied in fake eyelashes to make different colored tails on mayflies, and I've singed panty hose to shape the transparent wings of stoneflies. Using fake fingernails, synthetic eyelashes, and pantyhose as materials, I often look more like a crossdresser when leaving a store than a fly fisherman.

I walked around the square dining room table toward the tiny room were Zac sat. I peered over his shoulder as he knelt beneath a desk pressed against the wall and searched through a Rubbermaid tub. He looked up, his hands still rummaging through the container, and pointed toward the kitchen. "Go grab you a chair."

Zac pulled a black plastic case from the tub, set it on the table, and adjusted the blinds until there was just enough sunlight to illuminate the desk. He unlatched the case revealing a metal contraption like nothing I'd ever seen pressed into thick layers of black foam. Pulling out each part, he connected the metal pieces and tightened screws and clasps until a gorgeous vise was stationed on the desk.

"Pretty nice, ain't it?" Zac asked, almost bragging, but definitely not snobbish.

"Hell, yeah. How much did that cost you?"

"It was about three hundred, but I had to pay a little extra to get a pair of midge jaws for it."

He ducked under the desk and went back to digging through the contents of the tub. When he found something he was looking for, he took it from the container with one arm and placed it on the desk, never lifting his head, steadily searching through the pile of bags and organizers. Looking inside the blue tub I could see all sorts of animal hides: rooster capes, hen saddles, squirrel tails, hares' masks, buck tails, and a whole pheasant—if PETA ever got hold of a fly tier, there'd be a disgruntled fisherman arguing on network news for sure. He placed strung peacock herls, a long coarse pheasant tail, brown and white goose biots, a clear plastic container with compartments full of various-size hooks, a bag full of golden tungsten beads, and a spool of gold wire onto the desk. With all of the materials he would need lying on the desktop, he snapped the lid onto the tub and pushed it back under the desk.

"I'm going to show you how to tie a Pheasant Tail and a Prince Nymph," Zac spoke teacher to student. My eyes were steadied on the size 12 nymph hook he clamped into the vise's jaws. A golden bead was already strung onto the hook and pressed against the down-set eye. I didn't say a word. Later, folks told me that most beginners start by tying a Woolly Bugger, a simple pattern with a marabou tail, a spun chenille body, and palmered hackle, but Zac was teaching me to tie the two patterns that we used most often, two patterns that would always catch fish. With the hook securely fastened in the vise,

Zac reached for a gray foam block with tools sticking out of the top. He grabbed a tarnished brass bobbin, spooled with 8/0 dark brown Uni-thread, held the dangling thread between his left thumb and index finger, and angled the waxed line around the hook. Wrapping quickly, he doubled over the thread, secured it to the hook, and cut the tag end with a pair of sharp sewing scissors. The bobbin clanked against the vise as he pulled the scissors away. He hadn't given me any instructions up to this point, but I hadn't missed a turn. My eyes sucked up every wrap of thread and instantly transferred the information into memory.

"Now once you got the thread on there, you want to wrap back to the bend of the hook," he instructed as his hands went through the motions of every step. "Once you got the thread to the back, you got to grab some pheasant tail." He grabbed the long tail, plucked a few mottled strands from the boney quill, evened the edges of the strands, and added, "and tie it in to make the tail of the nymph."

Holding the thin ends of the coarse strands tightly between his fingers, he eyed the length of the nymph's tail and began wrapping thread around the base of the bunch, the white line which had held the strands to the quill still attached to the thickest ends. He whipped tight wraps around the pheasant strands, the thread cinching down the material as the wraps moved up the hook shank. Leaving the tag ends of the strands sticking straight up off the hook, he released his fingers and revealed the hairy tail of the nymph.

"When you got the tail on, you want to wrap back down to the bend and tie on some wire for the ribbing." He twirled the bobbin around the clamped hook, the thread quickly wrapping back to the bend. "Now some folks like to tie on the wire first, but I always done it this way and there ain't no need to change now." He grabbed the spool of copper wire, rolled out a two-inch piece of thin metal and clipped it.

With the strip of copper wire parallel with the hook shank, he spun a few quick wraps around the wire with the bobbin, securing the malleable metal, the wire sticking straight off the back of the fly past the tail and wobbling over the material clip on the vise. "Then you move the thread up the shank and start wrapping the rest of the pheasant tail up to make the abdomen." Zac grabbed the pheasant tail strands, the ones that stood straight up from the hook like a few sprigs of hair standing on a kid's cow-licked head. I still sat quietly, occasionally sipping the dark beer, which had grown warm.

Zac pulled the pheasant tail down to the underside of the hook with his right hand and began turning the handle of the vise with his left index finger. The rotating cam on the vise turned the strands around the hook shank as Zac created the tapered abdomen. With the fat abdomen constructed, he wrapped the thread around the pheasant tail strands and cut the tag ends.

Zac was skipping steps now, not telling me every detail, and assuming I was picking up the gist. He felt no need to tell me to tie things off or to trim the tag ends. His mind was on cruise control, doing what he had done a thousand times before, his hands going through the motions almost effortlessly. I swallowed a big chug of beer, finishing off the glass.

Once I'd learned the basics of tying from Zac, I learned to apply the techniques to other patterns. After I'd been tying flies for a couple of weeks, I could pump out certain patterns with considerable ease—not to say that my hands could whip finish a Royal Wulff while I watched TV, but with time the process took less concentration. In John Gierach's *Trout Bum,* he talks about having to tie 160 dozen flies, all of the same pattern. Gierach was tying flies to pay the bills, but still—160 dozen, that's 1,920 flies, all Adamses!

Gierach said that he never got into cruise control until after the first couple dozen. He said that by the time he got to that point, his fingers automatically angled wings perfectly so that when he tightened the thread, they would be positioned identically to the fly before, each fly mirroring the last one out of the vise. I've never gotten to that point, but I have learned where to place materials so that they turn perfectly when tightened by the cinch of wrapped thread. To be honest, I don't know if I'd want to get to the point where I'm tying 160 dozen flies. Hell, I haven't tied 160 dozen flies in the entire five years that I've been tying, much less that many of the same pattern. Gierach made his passion his work. Although I completely understand his desire to do so, I don't think that's a point I'm willing to get to. For me, fly tying has become more therapy than anything else. Tying is a practice that has a definitive beginning and end. I start from the bend and attach materials until I get to the hook eye, at which point I cut and am done. In a chaotic world of perpetual brain teasers, I need something that doesn't require much thinking, something with a product that I can see, touch, hold, and use when I'm finished. The satisfaction I get from tying patterns to mimic drowning stoneflies, emerging caddisflies, and flashing minnows is something that further connects me to the place I'm in love with. My enjoyment doesn't stem from any monetary gain, but rather connects to a firmer immersion into the wild. My flies mimic the bugs that fascinate me on the water and, hopefully, I create the trout's next meal.

"You can move pretty fast. How many flies can you tie in an hour?" I asked, amazed by how smoothly Zac's hands worked from bend to eye.

"Ah. If I'm in the zone, I can probably kick out about a dozen or maybe fifteen if I'm really flying. But on a day like today, I ain't quite sure. It should take me about six minutes or so, but the time starts going downhill the deeper I get into a six-pack or a bag of weed."

I was amazed at the time, but now that I've been tying for four or five years, I'm even more stunned. I can still only finish one every ten or fifteen minutes. Zac really was a master of his craft. He could wrap tight bugs with the best of them, but he was even more amazing on the water. Even as I broke his routine and asked questions, his hands never quit working. He probably could have done it blindfolded.

Zac once told me that he used to tie flies without a vise when he worked in a fly shop in Morganton. He and his peers would challenge each other to see who could tie the best whatever without a vise, with only their fingers pinching the hook. Now, I never saw those flies, but I imagine that they still looked better than my first couple of attempts.

"Now, once you got the thorax done, you'll want to grab the wire with some hackle pliers and wrap it up the thorax. This'll give it some weight, a segmented body, and some flash." Just as fast as I had gotten a word in, Zac was back to teaching. He held the wire tight with the pliers beneath the fly and used the rotary cam to wrap perfectly symmetrical bars of copper wire up the pheasant tail thorax. With the wire tied down at the same point where he had trimmed the pheasant tail fibers, he clipped away the excess.

"The next step's probably the hardest. You got to take another bunch of pheasant tail and tie it in so you can make the wing case, but the hard part is measuring it out so that the ends are long enough to make the wings."

I didn't have a clue what he was talking about, but I watched as he pulled away a few strands of pheasant tail and measured them against the abdomen and tail of the fly. He didn't tell me how to measure; he just went to tying the strands in, the tapering edges angled back toward the tail, the thicker tag ends immediately cut off.

He grabbed for a plastic Ziploc bag that contained the strung peacock herl and plucked a few pieces from the white twine that held the clump together. The peacock herl's iridescent hairs glowed green, yellow, and blue as the thin feathers twisted in the light. I've read that the iridescent plumage of birds such as peacocks and hummingbirds is not actually colored at all, but rather is clear with spaces within the hairs that refract light like a prism. Whatever the case, those strands of peacock herl put on a lightshow in the August sun.

"As far as I'm concerned, this is about the best material you can use on a fly," Zac informed me. "See all them colors? Trout love that shit." Zac's squinted eyes, still half-baked from smoking pot, opened a little as a smirk spread across his slender face. "This stuff'll make a fly dressier than a ten-dollar hooker on Broadway." He laughed.

"Now you use this to make the thorax," Zac instructed as he tied in the small bunch of herl above the pheasant tail strands. "I like to make my thorax big 'cause I tend to believe trout are more apt to bite a fly with a big profile."

He spun the herl thickly around the shank, making a plump belly on the half-finished fly. Then he tied off the herl just behind the golden bead head and trimmed the excess from the hook, the snip of scissors cutting hair sounding softly.

"We're almost done. Just got to make the wing case and the wings." Zac pulled the pheasant tail fibers (which till this point stuck out behind the thorax) over the herl, the fibers layering a thin line of mottled brown on top of the glowing green herl. He wrapped the thread over the pheasant tail, securing the fibers just behind the bead, and spread the tag ends with his index finger.

"All you got to do is spread these pieces of pheasant tail to both sides, pinch them back, and tie them down." His instructions made it sound much easier than it looked. His fingers quickly spread the strands evenly to both sides and pushed them back. Before I could blink an eye, Zac had wrapped the wings down, let go of the bobbin, and the shining jaws of the vise held a perfect Pheasant Tail Nymph.

The first time I caught a trout on a fly that I'd tied, I was fishing on Caney Fork Creek. Attached to my tippet were a broad-winged Stimulator, the elk-hair wing sprawled out like a porcupine's quills; and a messy-looking Prince Nymph, the wire ribbing loosely spiraling around the peacock herl body, and the white biot wings rolling on the body when I twisted the materials against the hook. Both of the flies were train wrecks, but I cast them anyway.

With the elk hair riding high on a seam of current, a native brook trout appeared off the pebbly bottom and engulfed the drifting nymph. I set the hook high into the fish's jaw and lifted the gorgeous mountain trout from the riffles. Something that I had created had looked enough like a meal for a fish to rise, feed, and be hooked.

The feeling of fooling a fish with your own design is an emotional experience that all too many fishermen will never achieve. When other fishermen are running a sharp point through the thin flesh of a night crawler, I'm cinching the knot on a Caddis Pupa. While bass fisherman hunt through shelves of brightly colored crankbaits, I'm wrapping furry dubbing on the thorax of a Golden Stonefly. Through fly tying, I've come to believe that these other means of luring fish to bite only distance the fisherman from the fish they love. Personally, I want to get as close as I can get, with my arm, the rod, the line, and the fly the only things separating me from the trout that I pursue.

"Just got to whip-finish some knots on this bad boy and I'll be done." Zac twisted the dangling thread into a triangle around an oddly bent tool and spun the knots behind the bead head. As he tied the last wraps of thread around the fly, the tight line securing the buggy Pheasant Tail Nymph reminded me of the last strands of silk being spun by a spider around a trapped moth. He cinched the wraps, cut the thread, and the fly was done.

"I'm going to put a little epoxy on the wing case to give it some shine, but that's it." I was almost brain-dead from soaking in so much information so fast. Although it's taken me a couple of hours to write out what happened, the actual event occurred in less than twenty minutes. Dumbfounded is not quite the word. I was a vegetable.

"Now you go ahead and try," Zac said, getting up from his chair and heading back into the main room. "I'm going to go roll a blunt. You just holler if you got any questions."

I switched seats and stared at the gorgeous nymph he had tied, the fly lying on the heavy pedestal base of the vise. There wasn't a chance in hell I could tie anything like that, but I put a hook in the jaws, grabbed the bobbin, and gave it a go. After a few minutes, Zac came in with the frosted growler, poured me another stout, and sat down beside me to eye my progress.

"Looks like hell, doesn't it?" I asked.

"Are you kidding? For your first time, that's a damn nice fly."

His encouragement was helpful, but I knew that his comment was merely something friends say in order not to break a friend's confidence. When I was finished, Zac helped me whip-finish knots to seal the job, and then I cut the thread. What hung in the vise was a scraggly bug with an uneven abdomen, loose ribbing, a thin thorax, and awful-looking wings. In the process of tying the fly, I had learned what Zac meant about measuring out the pheasant tail to make the wing case and wings. I had overshot my measurement and had to trim the excess from the wings, which gave them a blocky, unnatural shape, unlike the tapered wings of Zac's fly.

"That thing ain't worth a shit," I fussed.

"But it'll catch a fish." Zac urged. "Now, do it again."

That fly had taken me at least forty-five minutes to tie, but in the end he was right. My Pheasant Tail would catch a fish and later, on the water, it did. After a couple more attempts at a Pheasant Tail, Zac showed me how to tie a Prince Nymph. Surprisingly, I was a lot better at that pattern than I was with the first. People later told me that a Prince is a lot harder fly to tie than a Pheasant Tail because you have to match up the goose biots, which are difficult to work with in the first place; however, my Princes turned out nice, and I caught fish on them as well. Now when I look at those first couple of flies (which I've stuck into corks resting by my tying desk) and compare them to the ones I've tied recently, I know that I was on point when I said, "Looks like hell." Then again, they did catch trout.

Zac reclined in the wooden chair by the fan in the main room and lit the end of a fresh blunt, while I sat in that tiny nook, hunched over his vise. The pungent smell of reefer crept over the threshold as I tied fly after fly, getting better with each one. The empty growler finally caught up to me and my fumbling hands were no longer sober enough to make precise wraps. With a belly full of heavy beer and five or six loosely tied nymphs in my jeans pocket, I headed for my dorm room across campus. There was no question I would tie again. All I hoped was that my next attempt would bring buggier imitations, flies that I could be proud of—meals for trout, fish-catching feathers, lies a brookie would believe.

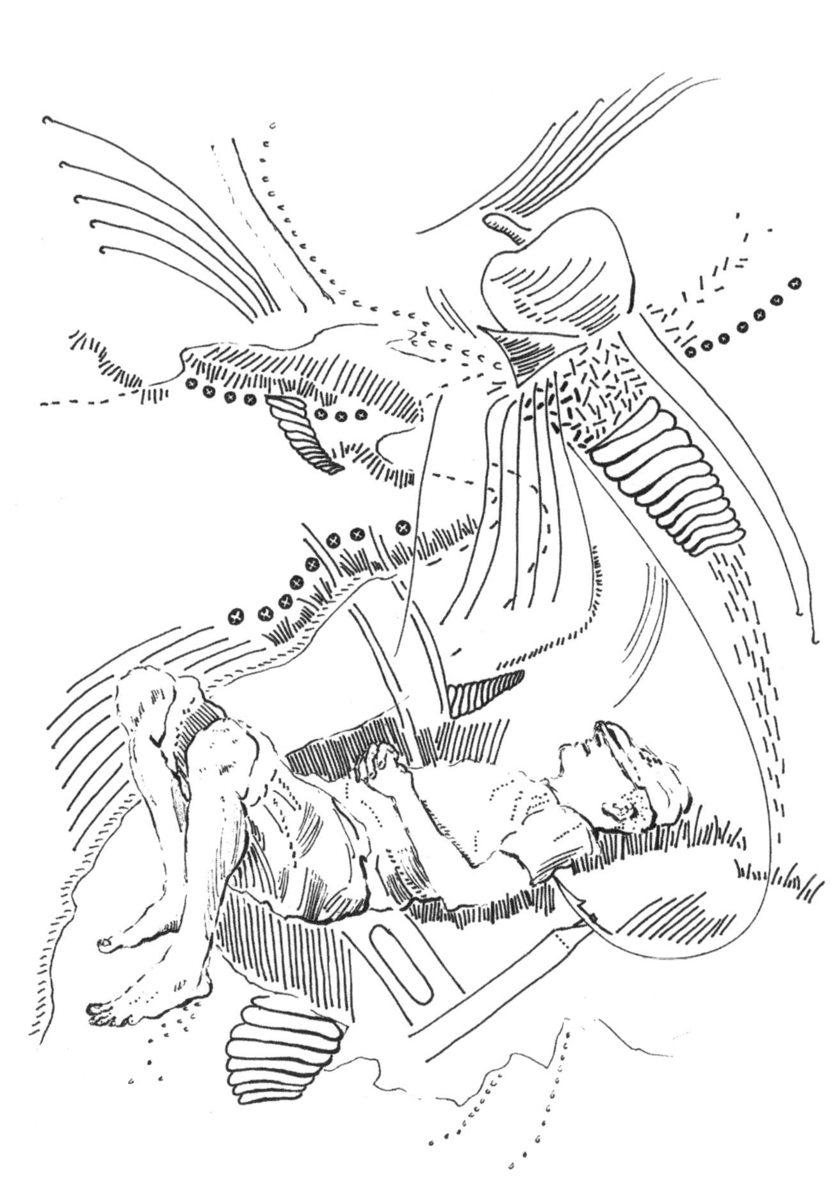

The Liar

The smell of freshly cut grass hung on the humid air of the July afternoon in Charlotte. Every man in the neighborhood had spent the Saturday grooming his yard. My father was no different, and he steered a circle into the grass with a rusted-out Murray mower. My job was to make sure rocks and fallen tree limbs didn't chop nicks into the sharpened blades of the riding mower. Dad mowed in a spiral, leaving one small patch of shin-high grass in the center of the backyard as he spun to finish. His head, with little hair remaining on top, was broiled red, his gray T-shirt was sweated to his torso, his glasses glued firmly to his nose, and beads of sweat glistened and rolled down every inch of exposed flesh. As the last blade of grass shot from the discharge chute, I had already predicted Dad's request and was on my way into the house to grab him a cold Cheerwine.

Almost three thirty and I didn't want to be late getting to the water. I grabbed my rod by the kitchen door and headed back out through the carport. Dad quieted the rumble of the small gasoline engine, and I handed him the drink.

"Thank you, son." Dad popped open the aluminum can and drank fast. I nodded and was already halfway across the yard when I heard him call. "Where you going?"

"Fishing with Darryl!" I yelled back, only turning for a brief moment to aim the words in his direction.

"Be back by supper," he said, but I was already gone.

The heat radiated off the blacktop as I ran toward the trailhead, a small opening in the woods on the right of the road. When I stepped onto the clay path, I could see Darryl up ahead standing in front of a large tangle of honeysuckle vine. Hidden from sight of the road and fathers, he was blowing cigarette smoke into the air, the cloud dissipating through the sweetness of summer. The burning cigarette was the last of a pack of promotional Winstons we'd stolen from a neighbor's mailbox. We didn't greet each other, he just passed the smoke, and we disappeared into the brush.

"I saw Ashley's tits earlier," Darryl proclaimed, his bird chest stuck out like a young robin's, his southern drawl mixed with remnants of his parents' New York accent. Ashley was a girl who lived down the road from us, one I teased viciously.

"Bullshit. You're such a liar." I flicked the finished Winston into a pile of damp leaves to the right.

"No, I swear. Her mom told me to go on up to her room, and when I walked in, there she was in the middle of changing." His eyes squinted as the smirk spread across his cheeks. "They were nice."

"What'd they look like?"

"You know, tits."

"Nice." This was the standard conversation of pubescent boys and one we knew very well. I wanted a little more description, something like in the letters we'd read in his dad's *Penthouse* collection, but didn't get it.

Darryl hopped over a small gulley, the remnant of a long-dried creek bed, and as his Voit high-tops hit soil yellowjackets swarmed up from the ground. Darryl took off and didn't stop, his allergic body knowing all too well the swelling of stings. He wasn't wearing a shirt, and all I saw was a blur of jean shorts, freckled skin, and the back of his coarse, black head as he continued flailing up the path. I walked around, keeping my distance from the angry wasps, and then sprinted to catch him. Jousting my rod through outreaching limbs, I caught up quickly, my long legs making up lost time. As he rounded the last curve and headed down the straightaway where the trail intersected with the barbed-wire fence encircling the cow pasture, he leaped over a thick branch lying across the path. Fifteen feet behind, I ran toward the branch, but at the last moment threw on the brakes and backpedaled to a stop as I noticed that what stretched across the trail was no limb.

A broad-banded copperhead was lying straight and still across the blend of clay and dried pine needles. The snake was thick, at least three feet long, and probably a male by the size. The tan body was lined with dead-leaf-brown-colored hourglass bands and was not shiny like the harmless blacksnakes we encountered often. The copperhead was dull and smooth like suede, and its triangular head was as large as a small mulberry leaf.

"Darryl! Look at this thing."

"Holy shit, dude, that snake is huge!"

"Yeah, and you jumped right over him."

"I thought it was a stick."

"Me too." I maneuvered around the danger, and as I got past, Darryl began prodding at the snake with the tip of his rod.

The copperhead quickly curled, struck twice in an instant at the tip-top, and moved off the trail. The thick pit viper nearly disappeared among the leaves and sticks. The snake was perfectly blended into the terrain. Its camouflage sealed a remarkable deceit to any prey. I've read that juveniles of the species use a vibrant yellow tail to entice frogs and mice to come close. The prey follows the lie and believes that the tail is a worm or grub, then wham!

Darryl was lucky that he hadn't been bitten. As the copperhead struck at the rod, its white mouth and fangs gaped visibly. We left it alone and headed across the fence to Johnston Pond, but the next passerby—squirrel, rat, or bird—would not be so lucky.

I felt I had witnessed two of the magical lies of the wild: the yellowjackets remaining hidden underground and the copperhead evaporating into the underbrush. Dangers were always out of sight but never out of our wary minds. Such a deception could kill young boys like us, and I thought Nature vicious to put on such a show; but looking back now, I no longer see it with such malice. The wild was no trickster. The wild was nothing more than exactly what it was. Everything was true. Really, there is no greater truth on earth than the reality of the natural world. Humans should dare to be so honest.

Vladimir Nabokov, the famed Russian novelist known for works like *Lolita* and *Pale Fire*, once wrote, "Nature always deceives. From the simple deception of propagation to the prodigiously sophisticated illusion of protective colors in butterflies and birds, there is in Nature a marvelous system of spells and wiles." Besides being a well-known novelist, Nabokov was a brilliant lepidopterist and his obsession with mimicry in butterflies often found its way into his other writings.

Nabokov's work with the Latin American blues (many of which are not actually blue in color, but rather orange) was particularly prolific. The South American *Chilensis* species is extremely toxic, eating plants known to sicken livestock, and many of Nabokov's blues take on bright shades of orange to mimic this species and avoid being eaten by predators. Similarly, the North American viceroy mimics the highly toxic monarch in color and shape. Nabokov deemed these wonders, "magic masks of mimicry."

As much as I respect the work and wonder of Nabokov's obsession with mimicry in butterflies, I shook my head at his seeing it as Nature's "deception." For me, the natural world is essentially truthful. Although the yellowjackets swarming around Darryl had seemed vicious, their hideout underground was no deception. The wasps were merely burrowing out of necessity, often needing to drag large prey to the colony when their wings lacked the strength to take to the air. These things were not done maliciously; rather, their assault was purely instinctual.

The same is true of the broad-banded copperhead. The viper was invisible on the leafy ground, but there was no conscious deceit. The mimicry of earthy hues was a phenomenal adaptation in order to remain hidden from prey. The wild was driven purely by raw instinct, thousands of years of adaptation leaving no need for cognitive deception. Humans are the only species who deliberately deceive. I wanted to do as Annie Dillard wrote, to "learn something of mindlessness, something of the purity of living in the physical senses and the dignity of living without bias or motive." I yearned to be wild.

At twenty-three, I trudged through a late spring current in search of rising rainbows. Late afternoon cooled the Tuckasegee River, but there was little activity on the water from bugs or trout. The few fish that came up gulped the surface briefly and then melted back into the river. The only sign a trout had fed was that brief moment when its snout broke the surface and the reciprocating ripples that died quickly.

Caddisfly hatches had been coming off every evening for the past few weeks and though a few scattered flies buzzed over the river, I saw no sign of the mass clouds I'd witnessed days before. I had no doubt that the horde would come, but casting was a waste of my time until the sun faded and the water dimmed. The sun was bright, the air was hot, and few insects were around to catch the eye of shifting trout. Under the shade of a hornbeam, I walked toward the shore and sat down on the tangled roots exposed along the riverbank.

A web of roots stuck out of the mud bank and easily supported my weight. I laid the fly rod at the base of the tree and stared down into the shallow water as the disturbed sediment from my footsteps began to settle. Through the glittering mica, I could see a pile of leaves and sticks layering the bottom. The shallow was a perfect place for caddis larvae, so I bent down and grabbed a handful of mud and debris. Sifting through the sticks, I found exactly what I was hunting for. It looked like three sticks glued together, the middle piece being a bit rounder, softer, and hollow—a caddisfly casing. The grublike larva had constructed a small home between the two twigs. The case was nearly identical in texture, shape, and color to the two sticks, but I knew otherwise.

Zac had shown me this variety of caddis larvae when we were fishing a small native stream. He called it stick bait and explained that he would occasionally use it when he was guiding to guarantee a client caught fish. I peeled the case in two, the consistency like heavy construction paper, and revealed the light green grub. Tiny legs extended from beneath the head, but the rest of the half-inch larva was all segmented body. I tossed the larva into the stream for the trout.

Lifting a nearby rock in the shallow, I found two more varieties of caddis casings attached to the underside of the stone. Both were tubular, but other than that, very different in construction. One was a bit larger and looked like a straw with microscopic pebbles glued all over the outside. The pebbles were all different shades and colors, and inside I saw the tiny head of the larva. The other casing wasn't round but had edges and was layered. It looked like a tiny watchtower, and the larva inside was smaller than either of the first two. I placed the rock carefully back into the river.

I was amazed at how well these insect architects blended into the world around them. The casings were probably invisible to most predators, and the larvae only revealed themselves when they dared to poke their heads outside. Their homes were sand and sticks, quite literally, and were absolutely unnoticeable to anyone who wasn't looking for them—a perfect adaptation.

Tired of waiting, I stood up from the roots, grabbed my rod, and sloshed out into the river. The 8½-foot rod brushed the overhanging leaves and limbs, and a swarm of caddis came down in front of me like blown ash. Some flew back into the foliage, some moved out over the water, and others drifted away downstream. I looked up and saw thousands of flies covering the branches. The gray caddis vanished if they didn't move on the bark. The green caddisflies were only visible by silhouettes on the leaves. They were all unbelievably hidden. The flies were awaiting the coolness of evening when they would take to the air again in one giant cloud. I watched them, holding tight to the hornbeam, for a long time. They were insects that moved like ghosts through all stages of life. The larvae built sturdy casings with spun silk and blended into the streambed. The adults held tight to leaves and bark and became phantoms of the springtime flora.

I thought again of Nabokov as I contemplated the marvelous camouflage of the caddisflies. The green caddis perfectly matched the color of summer leaves and the gray flies blended into the shade of bark. I wondered when the split had occurred, when the adaptation had brought about different colors in the same species. Their hues were an amazing defense mechanism, driven by inherent instinct and natural selection but were definitely no deception.

We humans rely heavily on language to solidify our world, and often we completely ignore our sensory perceptions. We look at a tree and see only a verification of the word, but a caddis does not know our meaning of tree. The caddisfly only knows which trees are good places to hide from predators; then they fly there and disappear.

Annie Dillard wrote, "The weasel lives in necessity and we live in choice.…I would like to live as I should, as the weasel lives as he should." How glorious it must be to "live under the wild rose as weasels, mute and uncomprehending." I go into the woods to try to escape the hypocrisy of my species. I catch glimpses of a life driven by necessity but soon fade back into what I am—a human and a liar. I think too much and live too little, but I yearn to revert to primitiveness—only then would I know what it is to truly be alive.

In early October I stood at the tailout of Caney Fork Creek where the water emptied into the Tuckasegee River, the two currents colliding and moving west. I'd waded in from East LaPorte in hopes of finding some big brown trout moving up the creek for sanctuary. The onset of fall meant the trout were just beginning to make their way into tributaries for the spawn. I'd seen a couple of fish holding on the sand where the creek entered the river, but the prospect of sex had them spooked.

Whoever lived in the trailer along the right bank had spread their home out under the Highway 107 bridge. The place looked like some shantytown of gypsies had set up a campsite along the riprap. Weathered folding chairs, empty bean cans and beer bottles, a small fire pit, and a clothesline supporting a dirty flower-patterned sheet were set up like a home away from home. Trying to enjoy the beauty of a trout stream in the fall, I found the sight a bit disturbing, so I tromped toward a large bend.

The creek was shallow with few ripples running over the collage of mixed stones. A large trout made a beeline up the shallow, the fish's back completely out of the water as it swam, the exposed dorsal slicing a V in the stream. To conceal my approach, I hopped up the riprap on the left and slowly stalked the trout. I'd seen where it had swum, but as I peered down from behind stalks of field grass there was no fish in sight. I made my way a bit further and continued peering through the sheen. Nothing.

I sidestepped down the embankment and back into the water. I was close to the bend now and positive the big trout must have kept moving for deeper water, eventually settling in the curve. I took a step upstream and immediately saw another wake as the same fish took off from the right side. I had looked over every inch of creek and must have run my eyes over that exact spot at least four times, but the fish had been there, invisible, and now was gone.

I was stunned I hadn't seen the trout. I'd stared down from directly overhead and seen nothing. I daydreamed of the cast I could have made, imagined the perfect drift and the trout taking the fly, but it would never happen. The fish was far more suited for the creek than I was, standing there like an alien misfit in green waders, leather boots, and a clanking vest. I couldn't have vanished if I'd been Eric Rudolph—the infamous abortion clinic bomber who hid in these mountains for five years before being caught—but the trout had no trouble disappearing.

I waded toward the bend and hoped the large fish hadn't spooked every other trout in the hole. A sandy mix of rock and mica created a beach on the inside of the bend. I crept on the shore and tried to remain low, unwilling to frighten any more trout. Kneeling on the pebbles, I made a cast to the head of the run. The Elk-hair Caddis bobbed through the curve and as it moved around the outside of the bend heading toward the tailout, a fish rose and took the fly.

I set the hook, felt weight, but not enough weight, and knew it was a different fish than the one I'd seen. This fish was not nearly as large, and as it made a run downstream, I felt only a slight resistance tugging the trout through the current. I moved to the water's edge and pulled the small fish into my hand.

In my palm squirmed a native that had come far down the creek. I'd caught hundreds of native specks farther up Caney Fork and in every tributary of the creek but had never seen so fine a fish this close to the river. I didn't know if a harsh flow from recent rainfall had sucked the marvel down or if the brook trout had another reason for coming to the river, but I didn't question it.

The color of a spawning brown would have been glorious to see, but a brook trout, in my eyes, was the cream of the crop. Gorgeous shades of green veined the top of the back and the season of fall was defined down the trout's belly. The colors were magnificently brilliant, but I wondered what the reasoning behind the adaptation was. Why did the trout turn these shades and how did it manage to disappear from predators?

I kissed the fish and released it back into the bend, but the questions continued. As I sat on the pebbly bank and hypothesized, it all began to make sense. If looked at from above, those green markings would disappear in the webbing of light being shattered as the sun came through the water. If seen from an angle or from below, the spawning brilliance would blend with the shades of the fall leaves and the sun. No matter which way the predator observed the trout, the brookie could disappear into its surroundings. Nabokov may have said that it was a "prodigiously sophisticated illusion of protective colors," but to me it was the perfect fusion of evolution.

In the trout's existence I found something that I wanted for myself. I was the only liar in the place, my Elk-hair Caddis a deliberate deception mimicking the hatch. I also had covered my pale skin with layers of clothes in natural hues in an attempt to meld with my surroundings, but it was obvious, at least to me, that I did not belong. I could never fully join the world that I loved so deeply. I was the species that dismantled the world with empty syllables, with metaphors meant to dominate. I wanted out. I wanted to become a fish.

I wanted nothing more than to shed my humanness like a snakeskin, to revert to a reality driven by instinct. I was tired of living in language-derived consciousness and yearned for moments without cognitive thought. I wanted to feel raw emotion—not to think—but just to experience it with my hairs standing on end, the pores beginning to sweat, my heart racing, as I was consumed by total fear. How pure it must be to truly experience the world even through fear! The only thing I wanted was to become what they were—wild—if only for a brief moment. Then and only then would I know what it was to truly be alive. Then, and only then, would I experience the rawness of the wild.

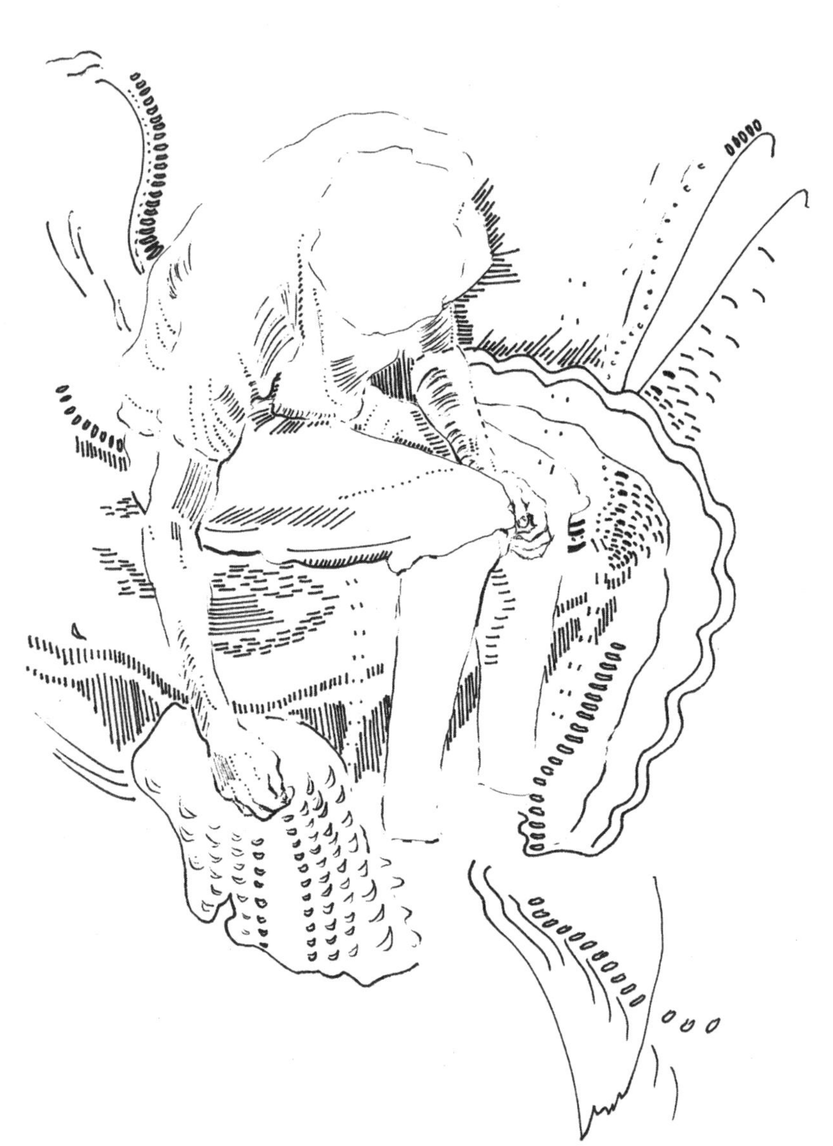

Wild

A breeze blows through a Carolina silverbell, showering its white bell-shaped flowers onto the mossy earth. One rattlesnake orchid grows in a damp corner of the creek bank, and beneath the flower's snakeskin leaves, a rabble of black and eastern tiger swallowtails suck moisture from the soil through uncurled proboscises like spiraled straws. I stand knee-deep in the crisp water and cinch the knot down on the hook eye of an Adams Trude.

The caddis hatch has been thick all day, and as the sun haloes the western peaks, the cloud of flies deepens into a gray fog over the stream. I pick my mark, make the cast, and watch as the calf-tail wing of the Trude slowly rides the surface along the seam of current. A brook trout rises, and I set the hook a bit too soon, only pricking the trout's olive green mouth. My heart pounds inside my sweat-stained undershirt. The moment of mistake has left me thought-less and I know that the fish will not rise again. More than the fish, that moment of thought-lessness was what I sought, and with my mind-scape barren, I climb the hillside and emerge on the gravel logging road. I look back down at Moses Creek one last time and find the line the trout had taken. I breathe deeply and deliberately, suck in every molecule of sweetness that the trumpet honeysuckles can spare, and then hike toward the truck.

On the way, my felt-soled wading boots brush a patch of bluets and the petals take flight. The flower patch transforms into a swarm of beating wings as the bodies of summer azures lift from the ground. I stop and let them spiral up around my legs and torso; a smile spreads across my face, and I am again thought-less. Not thoughtless in the sense of carelessness or insensitivity, but because nothing else exists besides the moment, a Ram Dass way of experiencing the "now." Fly fishing becomes my LSD, my meditation into existence. Nothing breaks the moment. I missed the fish, but I am not disappointed.

For me, fly fishing has become more than just catching fish. Yet it is too simplistic to say that it is an escape. In all honesty, I am not escaping anything. Rather than escape, fly fishing is a medium of becoming. A means of becoming animalistic, it is about a positive regression to primitiveness. As humans, our entire existence is defined by language, and language is the key difference between primitive instinct and cognitive thought. By breaking through all language-derived thought, I am able to revert to my primal self.

When these moments are achieved, language is out of place. I do not speak because I am too busy listening. The wild has no systemic, lingual tongue, only a dialect that can never be fully understood for anything other than what it is: wind on leaves, rustling; unseen birds' calls echoing off silence; the slight glup of a wild trout rising; water pouring over rocks; phantom animals brushing through rhododendron; my breathing.

The flowers are still defined by words and the birds still separated by empty syllables, but during brief moments of wildness these confines vanish for me and nothing is left but basic instinct: smell, sound, sight, touch, taste. For animals, there is never anything besides the moment. Primitiveness is not savagery. I want to return to Rousseau's noble savage: only then do I know that I'm there; only then do I become real; only then do I exist.

With the morning sun rising behind the jagged leaves of an Allegheny chinquapin, I approached a short, shallow run in the creek. A log lay on the right side of the current, and I was sure that a fish would be holding on the left of the fallen tree. I glanced to the left of the stream and saw a meadow of field grass through a thicket of briars as I took another stealthy step upstream. Edging closer to the line where I knew a fish would be holding, thought-less and in tune, I readied the fly line to make a cast.

Suddenly something burst through the briar patch on the left and came right toward me. The flapping intensified—something big. I turned and saw a wild turkey flying right at me. "Holy SHIT!" I screamed like a baby, high-pitched and piercing, the sound breaking the silence, my moment of instinct ceasing as I reverted back to my lingual consciousness.

The big jake took flight, flapping a six-foot wingspan at my head. As the bird flew forward, it slowed, outreached spurs aimed at my face, and hovered for a moment like a mockingbird attacking a hound. I swatted with my fly rod, grazing the jake's left wing, and a few feathers ripped from flesh fluttered toward the current. The turkey landed three feet upstream, then took off across the creek and up the hillside.

I thought that would be the end. I've seen hundreds of turkeys, generally hens, in these Appalachian woods, and every time the birds flashed a few short strokes and then ran for cover. I'd seen a bobcat burst from hiding and chase a raffle of hens across a logging road. Even then, the birds disappeared, gliding down a steep embankment without a feather spared. Evidently, my previous encounters hadn't taught me everything in a turkey's nature because this jake turned back toward me.

His head raised, his chest swelled, he exposed his long coarse beard, fanned out his tail, and gobbled loudly before ducking his head and dragging his wings across the ground as he came after me. I dropped the fly rod into the stream and reached into the water, picked up a smoothed rock the size of a mason jar, and prepared for the attack. The jake ran down the opposite bank and across the creek, about ten feet upstream from where I was standing. In the thicket, the turkey swelled again, iridescent plumage shining through briars. I was taken over by primal fear; fight or flight kicked in, and I don't have wings; I've never been much on running either.

In a moment of instinct, I lofted the rock over the thicket and, to my surprise, struck the jake in the breast. The thud was loud as bellowed air escaped from his chest. In that second of primitiveness, I had left the language-defined realm of humanity and become wild. I was thought-less. The turkey didn't fall but quickly scattered in zigzagged lines up the mountainside. I watched as he disappeared behind a patch of boulders. He would not be back.

Fly fishing can serve as meditation through which I can occasionally achieve complete consciousness, becoming fully aware of the moment. Oppositely, instances arise that thrust me so hard into primitive instinct that I immediately understand the steps my species has taken in our evolutional path. When the turkey attacked, I had no cognitive thought but shot immediately into survival mode. I have come to understand that moments of fear are one of the few catalysts for reversion. Faced with fright, I instantly go back to something deep inside, something not driven by language but guided only by the instinct of kill or be killed.

Animalism is much harder to achieve through meditation, taking hours to fully come into, and at times never occurring. Fear, on the other hand, forces you to become wild. I don't know whether one way is better than the other. Meditation is much more rewarding because of the lengths to which I must go in order to achieve those moments. However, the instant reversion to primal instinct seems more organic and reminds me of what I once was. The remnants of evolution are buried deep, but moments of fear light the fuse and I erupt.

A year prior, on the same creek where I was attacked by the turkey, the embers burned low as the night cold set in. It was late summer, but frost still covered blades of grass each morning. I crawled into my tent, opened the sleeping bag, and climbed into the goose-down cocoon. On the hillside, something rustled through underbrush. Too small to be a bear. Probably just a raccoon, opossum, or rabbit; but the sound was still enough to make me sit up and contemplate what was out there. I opened the tent, stepped outside wearing nothing but boxers, and chucked a rock where the noise had sounded. Then the night was silent, out there.

Out there. The idea of nature as outsider began to roam around in my mind like a feral hog searching for acorns. As I went back inside my tent, I wondered where it began and why early humans had felt the need to separate themselves from their animal relatives. Why did I feel the need to separate myself from the wild by enclosing myself in a thin nylon dome? As the night progressed, I drifted in and out of sleep, awakened periodically by scattering feet, wavering leaves, and an uncomfortable root that dug into my back. Finally, I gave up. I opened my eyes, adjusted to the dim moonlight illuminating the blue tent cover, and just sat.

I sat there all night, wanting to know why we go to these places, why we enter the wild only to separate ourselves in the comforts of civilization. We want to be there—we just don't want to *always* be a part of it. I wanted to climb a tree as my primate genealogy suggested, erase my civilized footprint, burn my tent, and stamp out the coals. Instead, I just sat there wondering, wanting, waiting; but the answer never came. The sun lit the inside of my tent at five thirty. The light bearer didn't rise, but glowed faintly behind the mountains, a lone candle behind a jagged black curtain. I climbed out of the tent and breathed in a mixture of hickory smoke and something indescribably fresh. Frost had laid down the field grass like parted hair, and my fly rod, waders, and boots shimmered with the dawn's touch. I sat Indian-style, poking at the blackened coals with a slim dogwood branch. Underneath, the embers still burned. I felt coals inside me, too, wanting air, waiting to flame into wildness.

Unwilling to wait, I slipped the damp waders over my pants, tightened the laces on my boots, pulled the fly vest onto my shoulders, grabbed my rod, and headed for the creek that murmured in the distance. When I got there, I dipped my hand into the frigid stream and wiped its cold water across my eyes. There wouldn't be any bug activity for hours, and on a creek this small no trout would rise this early. So, I just lay on the bank, the sandy gravel my mattress.

Birds began to call from branches, and slowly the sun ascended behind the peaks. It grew lighter but I still didn't move. By nine o'clock, I could see cumulus clouds sliding above the foliage. A caddisfly landed on my cheek, waking me from my trance. I stood up, stretched, grabbed my rod and dried my fly, and headed to a small pool where I had cooled my beer the night before.

I stood there for a minute watching the falling water aerate the head of the pool. My mind flashed back to the night before when I had sat on a stump staring into the fire. The glow of the flames had encircled my body, closing off what was outside, separating me from what I yearned for. Did our separation begin with the discovery of fire? I wanted to know: is this as close as it gets?

Even now as I stood above the pool, I was separated by my Gore-Tex waders, leather boots, and graphite fly rod, all unneeded modern conveniences, but also my most accessible means of getting close. I put Gink, a floatant for flies, onto the calf-tail parachute of my Adams and cast the fly into the pool. The incoming current pushed the fly into the far corner of the hole. As the Adams Parachute caught the outside edge of the seam, a trout rose to the imitation. I watched the fish come up on the fly, and as I did, all of my thoughts and cares drifted away downstream. My mind was empty as I set the hook and felt the pulse of the fish tugging on the tippet. I lifted a beautiful twelve-inch wild rainbow from the water and held the fish in my hand. For a brief moment, I was exactly where I wanted to be: thought-less and wild.

I wondered if wild was even the right word, considering it gave a negative connotation of something uncontrollable when nature should really just be. What's wild, in the truest sense of the word, is how land has been parceled and skyscrapers built, creating a world where peregrine falcons stalk from buildings rather than treetops. Maybe we've come too far.

I kissed the gorgeous rainbow trout on the nose, took in its sangria-colored lateral line peppered with black specks, and then released the fish into the stream. I knew the trout was born, had grown, and would die in that same stream; and I found something incredibly beautiful in that. The answers to my questions were no longer important as I watched the trout glide back into the riffles where it belonged.

UNTOUCHED

Tin roofs shone like shattered mirrors spread across the mountain range. The land didn't seem parceled around the homes like most development nowadays, and I probably wouldn't have even known the houses were there if the roofs weren't reflecting the midday sun. I drove toward a creek that I'd never even heard about. All that I knew of the water came from a blue line that wove across a topographic map. I often closed my eyes, ran my index finger across a flattened page and found the nearest creek on the atlas. Today as I headed for Beetree Fork Creek, I had no clue what to expect.

I estimated the drive from Cullowhee at an hour, but an ninety minutes into it, I realized that mountain roads could be deceiving in a book. I didn't complain. The drive was strangely exhilarating, winding through unfamiliar hollows where overhanging trees scattered the late-August sun across the rough pavement. I felt like an explorer on the hunt for new land, only I wouldn't exploit the wild. I would find a place, love it for what it was, and keep my mouth shut.

An orange-breasted robin flapped sporadically over the pavement and chased a tiger swallowtail. I rounded a curve where water trickled from a tall granite face cut into the mountainside to make way for the road. The mountain air felt wonderful against my sunburned skin. It was late summer, miserably hot on flatland, but deep in the Appalachian peaks, the temperature remained cool, chilled by streams, shade, and elevation.

Coming out of the bend, the road dropped, and at the bottom of the hill, I could see a man standing on the back of a harrow being dragged through turned soil by a fat-bellied mule. The mule's head bobbed as its hooves pushed through the loose dirt. When I reached the field, I slowed down to get a good look at the old timer. I couldn't discern his age (hard lives tend to wear on appearances), but if I had to guess, the man was around sixty. He held onto one of the plow's handles, reached into the back pocket of his beaten overalls, pulled out a red bandanna, and wiped the beads of sweat from his brow. The image looked like a scene out of a movie or a character from a Flannery O'Connor story, only there he was, close enough to touch.

Ragged wood posts lined the property, and rusty barbed-wire dangled between each post like bowed twine. Honeysuckle vines twisted around the posts and coiled out along the wires, the leafy plants converging in the middle of each wire. A black crow cawed from atop a post, and the bird's iridescent plumage shimmered blue and purple in the sun. The bird watched the farmer, glided down in the freshly plowed path, grabbed a churned-up worm, and flew away into the trees. Nature and man seemed to fuse back together there, making it hard to decide where one ended and the other began.

Past the field, the farmer's house sat at the bottom of the hollow, nestled below a steep hill. The house was sided with hardwood planks worn gray with age. A metal pipe bellowing hickory smoke stuck from the rusted tin roof. Knowing it was too warm to need heating, I thought that the family was probably still using a woodstove to cook meals. A rafter of wild turkey hens strutted in between grazing cattle on the hillside behind the house. White painted bee boxes lined one edge of the property, and I remembered the belief that when a beekeeper dies, someone must inform the bees or else they will leave. I wasn't sure who would tell them if that old man didn't wake up in the morning. Some folks are born at the beginning of a long row to hoe, but looking at how perfectly the man fit into his surroundings, I wondered if that saying was necessarily a bad thing.

The farm disappeared from my rearview mirror. The glimpse of the olden days, the type of life Granny told stories about, was gone, vanishing in the distance just like everything else. Gassing the battered Chevy up the next ridge, I turned up the bluegrass. Mandolins, dulcimers, and banjos twanged from the speakers, and I drove on—only a few more miles to go.

The older I get, the more I notice that the places become just as important as the fish I catch there. In the beginning, I didn't really care where I found them; all that really mattered were the trout. Nowadays, if I can't find a stream not bordered by houses or a place where I'm not bombarded by other fishermen, then I would rather not fish.

I find sanctuary in places unscathed by development, naked of human footprints, places where the wild remains. I read about West Virginia, Kentucky, and Tennessee where over eight hundred square miles of mountaintops have been flattened, the million-year-old rock blasted into dust clouds. Twelve hundred miles of streams have been polluted by runoff and over a thousand creeks buried. I wonder what happened to those mountains' farmers, their rich Appalachian heritage, their essential wildness? I wonder if my mountains are next.

I hear stories of rainforests disappearing in South America and ice caps receding at both poles, but the destruction doesn't become real to me until I see a multimillion-dollar home plopped beside a creek that used to hold native brook trout. Environmental destruction doesn't consume me until I watch a stream I've fished for years be strangled with sediment pushed into creeks by bulldozers.

I banged the steering wheel with my fist and drove on. The road darkened as I motored downhill and listened to chatters and screeches that echoed from invisible sources hidden in thick woods dense with briary underbrush and hazed with fog. I tried to identify what I was hearing, but without seeing the animals, it was hard to tell.

Aside from the road, there was no sign that people had been there. This was no tourist attraction, no highway lined with billboards erroneously portraying the Cherokee as Plains Indians. I tried to imagine that this place was exactly how it had always been. I wanted to push the fact that this was all new-growth forest out of my mind. I wanted to think these animals had no fear of man, that they'd yet to encounter the sputtering smoke of earthmovers; yet, the road was a constant reminder that I could never fully get back to what was.

As I emerged from the thick grove, a red-tailed hawk shot low across the road ahead. I wondered if a chipmunk, rabbit, or mouse hid in the patch of clover to the left. The land began to flatten out, and up the road, a concrete bridge crossed a deep gulley. The sound of water became evident, and I suspected I'd finally arrived.

I steered the truck over onto a small gravel pull-off after the bridge. I didn't see any tire tracks in the dirt, so I figured no one had fished that section in some time. I was two hours from home—a long drive but definitely worth it. I stepped out of the truck and heard the purr of water over rocks. That sound, more musical than chords from instruments, beckoned me to come. I pulled on my waders and laced my boots. I was anxious to get in the water. I threw my vest around my shoulders, grabbed my rod, and headed for the stream.

Pink rhododendron blooms were scattered under the thicket of trees, and a small path ran down the embankment between the bridge and the rhododendron. Midway down, Turk's-cap lilies sprang from the ground, with petals rolled upward toward sparse sunlight. The creek was gorgeous. The freestone bottom looked like a cobblestone street beneath a foot of moonshine. The water was so clear I could make out caddisfly casings stuck between rocks.

I knelt down beside the stream and began running my leader through the guides of my rod. With the tippet through the tip-top, I laid the rod on the ground and began rummaging through my vest for a couple of flies. No bug activity made it hard to choose which patterns were most suitable, but when in doubt, I always go with an Adams and a Pheasant Tail. Those two flies have caught me more fish than anything I've ever tied to my line. Sticking with my old faithfuls, I cinched a Uni-Knot onto the Adams Parachute and then tied the Pheasant Tail off the dry's hook bend.

I stepped into the cold mountain stream and wiggled some line out of the end of the rod. I read the water, trying to decipher the new creek to discover where the fish would hold—not that trout behavior differs much from stream to stream, but often they may hold more in runs on one creek versus pockets on another. A perfect eddy pushed to the right behind a large piece of shale, and a shallow run emptied into a pool upstream. I hadn't made my first cast, but I knew that there would be fish.

Fishing has taken me to the most beautiful places that I've ever seen. I've watched pelicans dive bomb breakers while I stood knee-deep in crashing waves, casting to pompano; I've seen great blue herons wade on stilt legs through hydrilla while I cast balsa wood bass bugs to largemouths; I've observed deer weaving through naked trees during the fall brook trout spawn; and I've gazed at a mother beaver guiding her young across the crosscurrent of a rushing river as I stood in a mayfly hatch casting to rising browns.

Fishing has taken me to places transfixed by time, places that remain untouched, places with the power to hold me motionless. Without fishing, I would not have the same respect and love for places wild. Yet, times on the water have taken me to other places that

I wished weren't there. I've stood in a boat anchored beside oil rigs and reeled in redfish, sheepsheads, and spadefish through oil slicks; I've watched a creek slowly fill with runoff until the water became shallow, raising the temperature, and forcing native trout to find new water. I've read about dams cutting off the yearly migrations of spawning steelhead, and I waited helplessly while developers clear cut miles of riverfront property, pushing wildlife away from their maternal waters.

I'm livid at the destruction and wonder how far I'm willing to take it in order to save one stream. I read Edward Abbey's *Monkey Wrench Gang* and envy his characters' reckless abandonment of the law. I want to sabotage those earthmovers and keep one stretch of land safe for a few more days. Sara and I turn Abbey's name into a verb and say, "We ought to Ed Abbey that lumberyard. We should Ed Abbey that development. Let's Ed Abbey those sons-of-bitches." Abbey's infamous character, Hayduke, is our hero, and we fantasize of disappearing into the night with the Monkey Wrench Gang. In the end it would settle nothing. This damnation, this whole damned nation, is completely out of my control, but I can't help feeling responsible just because I'm human. When I return to the water, cast my line, and observe all that is around me, I'm filled with an undying appreciation for these wild places and assume a responsibility to try to stop them from disappearing.

I headed upstream on Beetree Fork Creek toward the eddy on the right and hoped a trout would be holding in the swirling current. With enough line off the reel to make the cast, I started waving my 8½-foot 5-weight, my flies shooting closer with each progression. In one final double-haul, thirty feet of lime green line rolled out above the stream, dropping leader, tippet, and flies softly on the outside edge of the pocket. I threw mends, trying to hold the Adams circling in the eddy while the Pheasant Tail had time to sink. The drift was natural but a fish never rose.

I made another cast, dropping the flies perfectly into the seam that pushed out on the left side of the eddy. The Adams rode high, calf-tail parachute sticking straight up like a buoy as the dry came downstream toward me. I stripped in line with the same timing as the current, drag-free, invisible tension, but again nothing. With the first hole showing no signs of trout, I waded further up the creek toward the pool below the shallow run along the banks. The only motions in the hole were soft ripples running straight down the center, the current funneling down from the head. If there were any trout in that pool, I knew they would be holding either on the outside edges of the current or directly in the middle of the ripples. I picked a spot, deciding on the left side seam, and made the cast. The Adams floated like a cork but fooled no trout. I fished every line. Nothing.

I followed the same approach on the shallow run above the pool to no avail. I wasn't sure if the creek was barren, if there was something unknown about that watershed, or if I was spooking the fish; but as I looked around, it didn't really matter. I hiked further up the creek, finally moving out of sight of the bridge and my truck. All that mattered was that I stood in a place surrounded by nature, with no signs of human passage besides the jingle of tools clanking on my vest and the soft swish of Gore-Tex as I waded up the creek.

Upstream a giant hornets' nest that looked like a papier-mâché piñata hung on a limb of a water oak stretched over the creek. Black hornets climbed all over the hive and swarmed through the oak's leaves. At first I was hesitant to get close, but as I moved toward the nest and stayed on the far side of the stream, I was awed by those insects: the way they attacked any approaching bugs, the way they followed me with their eyes and repositioned themselves on the nest to watch me, and the way they seemed to systematically come out, one by one, flying off to pollinate a forest of wildflowers. I thought about coming back in the winter when the hornets were dormant and taking the hive home, but I couldn't take anything from a place so perfectly untouched.

I watched chipmunks chase each other around the loose bark of a cedar. I lay on a mattress of moss and stared up through the layers of leaves at fingerlings of blue sky. I followed the tracks of a raccoon that had searched the sandbars the night before. Eventually, I did catch a couple of native brook trout, but that was unimportant. I was happy just knowing the fish remained, that there was still cold water for the trout to fin through—knowing that the place was still wild was enough for me.

I stayed in those woods until encroaching darkness forced me back to my truck. Even then, I never wanted to leave. I hiked back with cicadas buzzing loud, then fading. Lightning bugs scattered bio-luminescent lanterns under the darkness of turkey oaks. Unseen animals began to scurry across the forest floor, and the dead leaves cracked under their tiny footsteps. When I got back to the truck, I slid my wet waders off, unlaced my boots, broke down my fly rod, and climbed into the cab. Everything was slower: my movements, my thoughts, the wind, time.

My biggest fear is that eventually, during my lifetime, there will be no more places like this, that eventually homes will take the place of wood groves, runoff will strangle the streams, peaks will be flattened into mesas, and the animals will disappear in a final failed exodus with nowhere else to go. People come to my mountains to escape urbanization, to see a place still holding onto its virginity, but with them they bring risk. The more people who come, the more roads that are built, the more homes that are constructed, the more these places vanish. When the wild is gone, we will be diminished. Cutting trees slices ourselves. Encroachment is our suicide.

I often think about what I would do if I hit the jackpot playing Powerball. The answer is always clear. I would buy every piece of untouched property I could afford. I would never cut a tree, never clear a plot for a home, just leave it the way it was. When I died, I would donate everything to an organization I knew would do the same; yet I know that even with twenty billion dollars, I couldn't buy it all. Places I have never seen would still be destroyed, and no one would ever see them again. Acreage around my home has risen in some places from $50,000 to over a $100,000 an acre. I flip through the pages of Jackson County real estate guides and wonder what the price will be for the last tree.

As for now, I fill my gas tank (an irony, I know) and drive as far as my wallet will allow, trying to find the few wild places that remain. I never pull into national parks; I leave those pruned refuges for tourists and people afraid of the wild. The parks are a valiant effort, but Aldo Leopold foretold the result. Parks bring roads, roads bring people, and people destroy solitude. In "Marshland Elegy," Leopold wrote, "Solitude, the one natural resource still undowered of alphabets, is so far recognized as valuable only by ornithologists and cranes." The same can be said for my mountains. Solitude is only precious to trout.

I search for places where trails have never been cut, where trees have grown from saplings to eighty-foot towers, where the jack-in-the-pulpits are still fresh with dew. When I finally find a place, I plant myself in soil, let the wild surround me, attempt to fuse with the natural world for just a moment, and then leave.

Back in my truck, I started the engine, rolled down the windows, and pulled out of the gravel. I bent down, temple touching the steering wheel, and looked straight up through the windshield. I could see the wisteria-colored sky with scattered stars beaming down like ancestral guardians. The road grew dark under the blanket of overhanging leaves. As I steered around a sharp curve, a red fox rushed across the pavement, its body low to the ground, its thick tail held straight out. I slammed the brakes to avoid hitting the small mammal. The fox never missed a stride, disappearing into the thicket of rhododendron and mountain laurel hugging the outside edge of the bend.

Further ahead, my headlights illuminated the *tapetum lucidums* (the mirrorlike characteristic in animals' retinas that gives the eyes that nighttime glow) of creatures hiding in field grass along the roadside and animals that held firmly onto the limbs of trees. I couldn't be sure what animal belonged to the glowing green pupils, but I enjoyed knowing they still had a place to hide.

I could see the old farmer's house in the distance. The windows shone yellow through the darkness, and as I approached I wondered what that tough highlander was doing in the early night. Driving past his home, I slowed down to peer through the windows hoping to see him. An orange glow grew bright on the front porch, the flame of the cigarette giving light to the hardened lines of the man's face. He was nodding back and forth in a rocking chair on the porch. I knew he was probably enjoying this place just as much, if not more, than I was. Certainly he was closer to this place than I could ever be. As I turned the corner past the farm, bats cut flips after fluttering insects spiraling through the cool night air right in front of my windshield.

I thought back on the few fish that I had caught that day. All were gorgeous native brook trout whose family tree dated back to the last Ice Age in the same mountains and the same streams. It hadn't been an active day on the water, but I smiled at sharing their refuge.

Almost home, I saw fluorescent lights break the darkness and knew I was back in "civilization." I wondered what it meant to be "civilized." Did it mean completely forgetting the sanctity of our primal roots, turning our backs on the earth that granted us life? A car's headlights began to show over the next hill like an electric sun rising over the horizon. As our headlights met, I saw a confused opossum trying to decide which way to move, trapped in the middle of the road. I slowed the truck and tried to give the animal an outlet, but the opossum went to the left and was smashed under the tires of the oncoming car.

I could have just as easily run over that opossum; I wouldn't have swerved off the road to save it. If it had been me, I would have been remorseful, but at the end of the day, I would have gone on with my life and probably forgotten. Forgetting our destruction is just easier. I try to force myself to remember, to always be aware of the effects of human life, but the cars keep driving, roads stretch further, and I am caught in the middle with the opossum, not knowing whether to turn right or left. Then I go to places untouched and remember. I make it to the other side of the road and disappear into the laurel with the fox. I escape the nighttime lights of civilization and converge with the darkness. My eyes can't glow, and I know that the animals watch me hesitantly even though I can't see them, but that's all right. At least I've made it to their side of the ditch.

"What in me is dark, illumine..."

My anticipation of leaving was clear as I rocked uneasily on the couch, sped through television channels, and knocked my knees together. Sara knew it but continued to make me wait. With the kitchen light reflecting against her jade eyes, she looked at me and smiled to offer some comfort, but I was antsy anyway.

"You ready?" I asked, sitting up to the edge of the couch, my eagerness evident in the loaded springs of my legs. I was a wad of stored energy, ready to explode at any moment.

"You said it wouldn't be worth fishing till eleven and it's only nine forty-five." Sara paced the hazy kitchen as she grabbed supplies to clean the stovetop, the smell of pork chops still hanging on the smoke of dinner. She was already dressed to go: ripped jeans, a gray hooded sweatshirt, and a windbreaker. Her dark hair was pulled tight into a ponytail. She had no reason to wait besides the pure enjoyment of watching me squirm.

"Yeah, but it takes thirty minutes to get there," I pleaded.

"Then we'll leave at ten thirty."

"How about ten o'clock?"

"Ten fifteen."

"Fine." She drove a hard bargain.

I looked at the rods resting against the armchair to my left and thought I'd better check the knots. I'd checked them at least three times already, but the urge to be on the water had my mind stuck on one track. I'd tied a Rooster Tail, an in-line spinnerbait that Sara had picked (real girly: black with sparkles along the shaft) from the rows of tackle at Walmart, onto the 6-pound monofilament of a spinning rod. The scratched reel held firm in the brass seat of my grandmother's rod, a rod with novels buried in the grip before I'd ever touched it, a rod whose story I continued with each cast, and now Sara would add her tale. She was unaware of the significance, but my letting her use that rod was a sure sign of how much I loved her.

I checked the knot on the Rooster Tail. Tight. Then I ran the line through my fingers checking for any nicks. Flawless. The rod was ready to fish.

A 7-weight fly rod rested across the arms of the chair, the perfect balance of rod and reel keeping it stable. I'd yet to fish this rod, an 8½-foot, 7-weight with a jet black Ross Rhythm held firm in the rosewood reel seat. I'd bought the setup specifically to night-fish for trout. I'd read the words of George Harvey, Joe Humphreys, and James Bashline on night-fishing for big trout, specifically browns, and built my rod to match the masters'.

Traditionally night-fishing for trout has been a northern habit, with the nighttime roots buried in the cold currents of Pennsylvania. Bashline's prose bragged of monster trout ripping drag to the backing, and the photograph of Joe Humphreys's 1978 Pennsylvania record brown, a gargantuan fifteen-pounder, spoke more than any number of words. The facts were simple: the biggest trout fed at night, and although the game was harder in the cloak of darkness, I wanted my shot. I had learned their northern techniques and wanted to apply the theories to my southern tailwater.

When the rod I'd ordered to night-fish had arrived, I'd eagerly waited for the next new moon. I marked the date on my calendar and loaded my fly boxes with recommended patterns (Mice, Sculpins, Harvey's "Pusher Fly," and classic streamers like The Professor) for that night.

Despite popular belief, big trout prefer complete darkness to the lantern-lit nights of a full moon. What means feeding frenzy for giant browns means something entirely different to the fly fishermen who pursue them—danger. I find it hard enough to wade the smooth rocks of a slippery freestone river in the daytime, but doing it at night can easily become a death sentence.

One of the keys to nighttime trout fishing is to target a fish that you've seen during the day. Casting to schools of dumbfounded stockers weeks before, I'd seen mine—a colossal brown trout. It easily topped thirty inches. I'd gotten a good look when the fish torpedoed through the surface to engulf a spinning mayfly just feet from my vantage point. Since then I'd watched the fish hold the same feeding line day in and day out. High water from recent rains made it impossible to chase the monster tonight. I wanted a chance for a trophy, but suicide was not on my to do list.

The Tuckasegee River was running too high to fish, so I'd decided to try Bear Lake, a deep mountain reservoir southeast of Cullowhee. Sara and I had scouted the lake earlier that day when we were planning where to fish. We had seen schools of fairly large trout swimming the shallows and some bigger fish moving among the shadows just out of casting distance. I hoped they might come into range when darkness fell.

An elk-hair Whitlock Mouse, a giant fly meant to mimic a drowning deer mouse, was tied to the tippet of the 7-weight fly rod. I checked the knot, rubbed floatant into the coarse hair of the fly, and ran the tippet and leader through my fingers. Everything was a go, and after ample begging, I talked Sara into leaving early. At five after ten, we were out the door.

Night-fishing was not something new to my résumé. I come from a long line of nighttime anglers, my father spending many nights jug fishing for channel catfish or spotlighting flounder to gig. As soon as I was allowed to stay out well into the night, I was casting from sandy banks, creaking docks, or anchored Boston Whalers to anything that would bite.

I'd caught fat-bellied channel catfish, coolers full of speckled crappie, schooling bass busting shad on the surface, and even a longnose gar, all under the cloak of darkness. I instantly fell in love with the feeling. Night-fishing was not a sight game but involved the sound of bait clickers running, a bump on the rod, a swift hook set into something unseen and unknown until the fish came to hand.

I longed for that feeling, the mystery of not knowing what it was that tugged on the end of the line. I remember standing on an abandoned dock in a North Carolina inlet when something picked up the squid on the end of my line, ran off two hundred yards of 20-pound test, and never looked back. I still don't know what bit that night, but that's just it—the mystery of the unknown is what drives me forward into the black.

Swerving through the bends of mountain roads, I felt fishing fever take hold. My mind raced, and my palms sweated as the addiction set in, the feeling comparable to an alcoholic denying himself a sip of rotgut after a weeklong drinking binge. The withdrawals wouldn't subside until the first cast. Sara was excited at the chance of her first real fish, but a lifetime of dependency was evident in my shaking limbs. The difference between us was obvious: Sara came from a family who occasionally dropped a line in water on vacation, but I was of a different breed, a family of fishermen, children who had been raised with rods in hand rather than crayons.

I sped toward water, the liveliness of summer becoming apparent as giant moths smashed against the grill and windshield of the speeding Chevy, the thuds still audible through the blare of O.A.R.'s "I Feel Home." A blur of bushy tail shot across the pavement as a red fox made its nighttime chase. Through a stand of jack pine on the right, the dirt road to the Bear Lake boat landing came into view, and we eased into the empty gravel parking lot, the unsettled dust clouding the road behind. I steered toward the boat ramp and parked under the fluorescent glow of a streetlamp, insects swarming the bulb, the light barely reaching the darkened shoreline.

"Will you grab the cooler?" I pointed to the passenger floorboard of the pickup.

"Sure, and what else?"

"I'll get the rest. You just grab the cooler." The beer cans sloshed in the icy water as she lifted the red Igloo onto her lap.

"Let me get something else."

"No, just get the cooler." I opened the door and stepped outside while Sara checked the hour on her phone one last time.

The smell of dead fish blended with the sweetness of barley grass and the sourness of Queen Anne's lace growing alongside the boat ramp, a repulsive smell to most, but a cologne reminiscent of nights on the Catawba for me. A little brown myotis bat shot low past the driver side, and I heard the velvety flaps of winged hands. I looked up and saw many more spiraling, flipping, dropping, ascending after the erratic flight patterns of nighttime insects.

"Bats," I called just as Sara began to step out of the truck.

"Where?" she yelped, looking up toward the light as one of the winged mammals flew low and cut off into the black. "Holy shit!" she screamed frantically, her feet breaking into some scared-shitless river dance, the door slamming behind her as she jumped, yanked, and shut the door in one clean movement.

I cracked the driver side door. Sara sat in the fetal position on the passenger side bucket seat.

"You know they'll lay eggs in your hair and you'll go crazy," I prodded her with lies.

"Shut up, David! That's not funny!" Her voice held a seriousness best left alone, but my comment had to be true—after all, I'd heard it from Barney Fife on *The Andy Griffith Show*, a true authority on life.

I grabbed the rods out of the back of the truck with one hand and picked up the old Plano tackle box and the fly case with the other. I headed toward the lake, stopped in front of the truck, and motioned for Sara to come on.

"Are they gone?" she yelled from the safety of the cab.

"You're fine."

"You sure?"

"You're fine, babe. Grab the flashlight, while you're in there."

Sara emerged, the cooler sloshing in one hand, the flashlight in the other guarding the crown of her head as she ran toward me, her petite frame wobbling from the weight of Busch cans and ice. We walked out of the circled light of the streetlamp and headed toward the glint of shimmering water.

The crickets and bullfrogs silenced as we neared the shore, and Sara shone the flashlight onto the planked dock lining the landing. We stepped onto weathered boards, the fasteners creaking along the posts as the dock shifted under our weight. I set the boxes down and handed Sara her rod. She cut the light and blindness set in.

When the lights faded and vision vanished, my other senses strengthened as I tried to make out what was left. Night blindness forced me to heighten my other perceptions in order to decipher the world around me. I felt the wind pushing from the east against hairs on my legs. I smelled the blend of yellow poplar blooms mixing with the water as the scents rode the breeze across the lake.

I heard a raccoon making its way along the bank to the right, the nocturnal hunter scratching the sand for buried clams. I could not see the trees that I smelled or the animals scavenging, but I knew they were there. Creating a world in my mind, I imagine the cast, the place where the fly will meet water, and I begin the motion, sending the Whitlock Mouse into oblivion.

Sara walked to the edge of the dock, the planks rocking with each step, and cast into deep water. I heard the Rooster Tail splash in the night and the spin of the reel as Sara brought the lure back to the dock. I started a backcast—careful to avoid the thick mix of alders, elms, and poplars on the bank behind—and sent the fly toward a point of riprap off the right side of the dock. The fly landed silently, the elk hair of the mouse pattern disturbing little water as the fly struck the surface. A loud pop echoed from the area where I suspected the fly had landed, and then I felt tension on my line. First cast and a fish was on.

The 7-weight throbbed at the tip as the phantom fish dug toward the rocky bottom. I couldn't know what was on the end of the line, but whatever it was had smashed the Whitlock Mouse as soon as it touched water. I reeled the fish toward the dock and asked Sara to bring the flashlight. I heard her set her rod down and walk toward me, shining the light onto the surface. I could see a nice-size rock bass still tugging toward the dock posts. I lifted the fish from the water and laid the bass on the weathered wood, the rough planks drying the scales of the fish.

As the rock bass lay on the boards, its crimson eye shone in the glare of the flashlight. The eleven-inch marvel—its brass-colored sides mottled in dark brown, the white belly, and golden pectoral fins rowing in the night air—was a vicious striker. The Whitlock Mouse was larger than the fish's head. The fly extended from its mouth, over the gill plate, and rested beneath the rotating pectoral fin. I questioned what a fish that size was doing eating a mouse, but its bass genealogy left little to be explained. These were ferocious game fish and they make delicious table fare. Only trout are too holy to be eaten as far as I'm concerned, so this fish was headed home with us.

I ran a nylon stringer through the fish's gills and out of its mouth, then secured the cord to a dock post. Sara cut the light; I cracked a beer; and she lit a joint I'd rolled for her at the house.

The fizzing hops and metallic taste of cheap beer in an aluminum can was a perfect celebration for the first fish of the night. The smell of reefer held strong around the dock, and I swallowed hard to get the beer from can to stomach as quickly as possible. I picked up the rod, swung the fly into my hand, and felt the wetted hair of the mouse. I secured the fly to the hook keeper of the rod, sat down on the dock, lit a cigarette, and stared up into the May sky.

"There's Orion," I said as Sara took another drag from the joint.

"Where?"

"Come here and I'll show you." She walked toward me, her face becoming visible briefly when she pulled on the joint. Standing beside her, I took her hand and drew lines in the sky. "You see it?"

"No."

"You see it now?" I traced the outline of the archer again.

"Yeah, I see it now."

She sat down beside me and smoked her joint while I finished my beer and cigarette. When the break was over, we went back to casting, the plop of her lure breaking the silence of the summer night.

We cast for the next hour or so, and eventually the 7-weight began to take a toll on my wrist. I sat back down and took another can of beer from the icy water of the cooler. I was sprawled out on the dock, elbows holding up the weight of my torso, cigarette dangling from my lips, beer resting to the right, when Sara shot to life. "I've got something!" she said, her voice giddy with her first fish on the line.

I sat up fast, accidentally kicked the unseen tackle box by my feet, and lunged toward her as I tripped down the dock. "It feels big!" She was becoming louder now, her shouts ricocheting off the softwoods lining the bank.

I could see the silhouette of the rod bouncing against the cobalt sky. Her small hands struggled to turn the reel handle as the fish put pressure on the spool. The fish slapped across the surface, ripples becoming visible as the stars glinted against the black surface. She reeled the small fish all the way to the tip-top of the rod, Granny's steel pole bowing to the weight. I grabbed the aluminum flashlight by Sara's shoes and shone the blue-tinted LEDs toward her catch. "That's another rock bass," I said in surprise.

"It's big, ain't it!" she said, her pride evident in each word.

"Yeah, it's pretty big." I tried to be as enthusiastic as she, but years on the water had depreciated my empathy for first fish trophies. The fish was around eight or nine inches, but what it lacked in size was made up with the same gorgeous coloration as the first. Its copper sides were brighter than my fish's and the eyes more blood red.

I snapped photos as she stood proudly on the dock. The developed pictures show a gorgeous young woman, bright-eyed as a child, smile spread across her cheeks, with a small rock bass dangling close to her face. We strung the rock bass next to the first, and Sara relit the extinguished joint, her own celebration of sorts.

While she sat on the dock, I picked up the spinning rod and started making casts along the bank. I hadn't fished with Granny's rod in a long time. When I'd moved to the mountains, I'd switched entirely to fly fishing and hadn't looked back, but with the heaviness of the 7-weight wearing on my long arms, the limber spinning rod felt good. I cast across the landing, reeling the spinnerbait above sunken riprap and over submerged concrete. As the line neared the dock, I felt weight. The rod wasn't slammed but felt like I'd snagged a log. Then the headshake told me otherwise. A fish was on, and it was no rock bass.

"Sara, get the light; there's something big on." She grabbed the flashlight and came toward me. "It's got to be a big brown," I guessed. Thoughts of the large trout that we'd seen earlier in the day lurking just out of casting range ran through my mind, then images of Joe Humphreys's trophy that he'd spent months pursuing.

The rod bowed to the water, the steel pole doubled over by the thrashing fish. This is what night-fishing is about—hooking into something huge and having absolutely no clue what in the hell it is. Sara shone the light into the clear mountain water, and I saw the monster shaking its head along the sandy bottom. I pulled up, drag ripping from the spool at the first sign of tension, the fish rolling its white belly into the light. The fish exploded through the surface, ten feet out from where I stood, and I reeled hard, knowing I had it as soon as it came atop.

"Hold the rod, Sara." I handed her the cork grip as I stretched across the planks and hung over the edge, trying to get close enough to grab the fish. Sara held the rod in one hand and attempted to shine the light accurately with the other. I reached down, the fish swiped madly, and I saw teeth, lots and lots of teeth, clamped around the tail of the spinnerbait.

"That ain't a trout!" I yelped, the large scales a giveaway that this was no brown.

"What is it?"

"I don't know, some kind of toothy bastard! But it's big!" I grabbed behind the head, while the large tail slapped furiously against the water. Gripping firmly, avoiding teeth, I lifted the fish from the lake and set it on the dock. The fish flipped over and over as Sara shone the light down on the greenish yellow body.

"It's a walleye!" The catch marked a new species on the totem pole of my life.

"I've never caught a walleye before."

"What's a walleye?"

"It's a fish that they go crazy for up north, but I've never even seen one in person. They're supposed to be damn good eating too." The light shone on the golden eyes of the walleye, the pupils opaque in the glare of the flashlight. The fish easily weighed six pounds and was at least twenty-four inches, a pretty nice size for a first walleye and a trophy for me.

I dug through the tackle box and pulled out an old rusty pair of needle-nosed pliers, the rubber grips dry rotted and peeling away from the handles. As I tried to unhook the fish, I saw that the treble hook of the Rooster Tail was stuck deep into the maxilla, a large bone along the back of the upper jaw. In the light I could see teeth coming straight out of the roof of its mouth behind rows of primary fangs. Indeed, this was one toothy bastard.

Sara lifted the stringer from the lake and brought it to me, her rock bass hanging lifeless atop my flopping first catch. I grabbed the walleye strongly behind the head, the sharp dorsal spines sticking up behind my grip, and noticed the fish's belly protruding below my curled fingers. It was a large pregnant female, full of eggs and heavy in my hand.

The thought crossed my mind to release the trophy, but memories of recipes for walleye in back issues of *In-Fisherman* forced the stringer through its gills. I held her up for Sara to get a good look and then lowered the stringer into the lake. The walleye yanked on the nylon cord as it sharked beneath the surface, the two rock bass being pulled to the side of her face. The one rock bass that was still alive flapped against the side of the walleye with bursts of inherent flight response.

Sara cut the light and the night was again black. I sat down beside the cooler and opened another beer. Sara picked up the rod and began to cast again.

"Ain't that just the way it goes?" Sara asked from down the dock.

"The way what goes?"

"Soon as you grab my rod, you catch that damn thing," she declared, the disappointment now made clear in her tone.

"I can't help that, Sara." I laughed under my breath, not wanting to hurt her feelings.

"No, but that's just how it goes."

I kept quiet, tried not to rub anything in, but damn, that was a nice fish. I was floating, but I didn't let it show.

Her casts became more determined now. Out of jealousy or spite, she cast faster and reeled harder, but nothing bit.

I lit a smoke, the smell of burning tobacco holding around my face, and listened to a fish break the surface somewhere out on the lake. A great horned owl hooted from a limb along the shore as I lay back on the splintery planks and listened to the whiz of Sara making another cast.

This was night-fishing at its best: a warm summer night, a new moon, a cold beer, a half a pack of cigarettes, and a damn nice fish on the stringer. I drank a few more beers, but not even the alcohol could numb the intense perceptions brought on by the darkness. The sound of another fish splashing in the water echoed across the lake. The hairs on my arms stood on end as the noise reverberated in my ears. I was experiencing euphoria on that dock.

I could have sat there until morning slowly spread across the waving water. But there were fish to clean, and I knew that dawn would only bring a bitter end to my sweet blindness.

Sound of Silence

Snow had fallen the night before in Jackson County and was supposed to continue all day, but in Cullowhee midday temperatures rose, melting white powder into muddy puddles and leaving nothing more than patches in the coolest shadows. The snow had turned to rain, and the plowed piles along the roadsides had been compressed into dense, smoke gray slush. I climbed into my truck, cranked the ignition, and waited for the engine to warm. I put the truck in reverse, turned onto Highway 107, and headed toward the creek.

Driving in silence, I hoped the snow was still falling on the highlands, that the fresh powder blanketed the naked peaks, brightened the dead browns of winter, and hung on the tree limbs like layers of thick white lichens. Having spent Christmas in Charlotte, I yearned for the stillness of the mountains, and although I knew the fishing would be difficult, time on the water is always time well spent. I could sink into a single place and time and become centered in the wild.

As I climbed, the precipitation slowly evolved: first rain, then sleet, and finally snow. The flakes came down heavy, and the barrage of snow pummeled around the Chevy. The snow never actually touched metal but zoomed in and passed in white lines like stars when the Millennium Falcon hit light speed. The yellow lines were barely visible, but I leaned forward, chin hovering over the steering column, nose close to the windshield, and drove on.

Caney Fork Creek ran beside the road, the dark current running black like spilled molasses, one thick line always moving onward.

Rocks that broke the surface were shelled in white humps. The world was a monochromatic pen-and-ink drawing, all blacks, whites, and grays in a blend of lights and darks: shadowy gray clouds, black creek, white snow, crosshatched bark of naked trees. Without distractions, I was able to focus on everything as a whole.

The plank board sign bearing the creek's name was almost buried, but I made the turn onto the gravel driveway and slowly eased toward the creek. Smoke bellowed from the tin flue on the house next to the stream. I parked beside a line of rocks supporting wood posts worn gray. Barbed-wire fence dangled between the posts, and the iced-over barbs looked like glass jacks strung along the rusted wire. The horse pasture was empty, but a mixed-breed mountain dog scurried across the blanket of snow toward my truck.

I cut the ignition and opened the door, the heat of the cab escaping as my skin was finally exposed to the cold mountain air, a good ten degrees cooler here in the highlands. If one word could describe the air, it was penetrating: penetrating my layers of clothing, penetrating my skin and bones, rattling my skeleton and waking me to winter's harsh reality. It felt good—nothing like an uncontrollable shiver to let me know that I'm alive.

A short-legged mutt stood at my open door, his body shaking, mouth panting, and tail wagging. His movement seemed to speed his heart and warm his muscles. I knelt down, stroked the spaniel-spotted coat, patted hard on the large black spot wrapping around his back, and stared into his eyes, one blue and one brown. I tried to assure him that winter is only a few months; that warmer days are on the way, my anthropomorphizing denying that the animal was better suited for the weather than I was. I gathered my gear and headed for the creek. The grinning mutt stayed by my side until my first step into the water, when he looked one last time and took off through the tangled underbrush.

I was alone now, exactly where I wanted to be, by myself with nothing but the wild. The creek meandered through the valley like a blacksnake, and cedars and balsams bowed toward the earth, the branches heavy with snowfall. The temperature of the icy water pierced through my thin waders, sweatpants, and long johns. The bitter cold was a reminder of my warm-blooded nature. But I chose the cold over the controlled warmth of a couch, glad to make the sacrifice. The long-awaited silence would soon bring me calmness.

I'd come to escape the ongoing noise of civilization. Every day I walk around in a world where people listen more closely for the electronic ring tones of cell phones than for the faint cries of soft-spoken bluebirds, the trickle of water over rocks, or the rustle of dried leaves still holding onto twigs of shaking limbs. The sounds of nature are drowned out by speakers blaring electronic riffs, so when someone would like to hear something wild, they buy the sounds on compact disc and call it something like "Tranquil River." Few take the time to just stop, hold still, and listen to what's around them. The world has become a place of synthetic sound, a deafening reality—the definition of noise.

The noise is a direct result of the rush. I drive on roads where forty miles per hour is a catalyst for middle fingers, blown horns, and curse words silenced behind windshields. Who's got time to brake and look at a blooming yellow poplar when closing time is in an hour? Everyone hurries to get some place that doesn't matter, to a place that will be there in the morning after the last leaf has fallen. People rush around with blood pressure boiling and aneurysms building until they need a prescribed fix. Rather than just taking the time to be still, they push themselves forward, each second another tick of wasted life. "Shorter of breath, and one step closer to death," Pink Floyd sang.

Personally, I can only wander through the modern world for so long before I feel the need to find places without people, without noise, without the frantic pace of modern society. I believe it is my disgust for what is happening to the environment that is associated with my noise phobia. I can tie it back to a moment when I heard the roar of a Bobcat tractor crack through a red maple I used to sit under every day. Now, the blended cacophony of machines angers me.

I must leave and find refuge in the trees, by a stream, or on a rock and then refuse to move. I hold tight to my sanctuary until I can stay no longer. God, how I envy people like Thoreau, Horace Kephart, and Annie Dillard. To just run away and find serenity in the woods, become a pilgrim on a creek—what a wonderful dream, but the reality is that I can't, at least not now. Another day, another dollar, another step toward the grave. Luckily I have places to hide, and right then, on that winter day, I was there.

Kneeling in the shoal of the creek, I strung my fly rod and searched through boxes for the perfect midge. I would have to fish small. I had no use for tying on a bug the size of a green drake. No insects were out on the water and wouldn't be for months. I knew that and the trout definitely understood it. The only forage for brookies in wintertime is a smorgasbord of tiny midges, larvae the size of arm hairs dancing in the frigid water. During the cold months, the entomology of a stream dwindles, leaving little more than chironomids (mosquito larvae) moving through the current. Yet thousands of the larvae can cloud a creek even during the coldest stretches of winter; and the trout wait, zero in, and snack.

I found a couple of flies hidden in the back of my nymph box: a Zebra Midge and a Biot Midge. The size 24 Zebra Midge—consisting of black thread, silver ribbing, a turn of peacock herl, a silver bead head, and antron-yarn gills—was an elaborate representation, a microscopic work of art. The size 26 Biot Midge, on the other hand, was simple: a dyed yellow goose biot wrapped up the hook and a tiny gold bead the size of a pinhead. Tiny hairs that had lined the outside edges of the biot stuck out from the segmented body of the fly, a perfect match to the naturals. Still, picking the flies was the easy part. Now I had to run tippet through the tiny hook eyes, with dim light and shivering hands, frozen red as tomatoes.

My stiffened fingers shook as I tried to run tippet through the eye of the Zebra Midge, but I finally got the flies on my line, attached a green strike indicator of braided poly-yarn four feet up the leader, and turned back toward the water. A spot of color caught my eye. I turned and saw a plump robin resting in the nook of a dogwood, his plumage fluffed out like a goose-down jacket. Unlike in the spring—chaotic with scampering footsteps, calling finches, and clicking gray squirrels—in the winter woods, all was quiet.

I was sure the trout were still there, that they finned slowly along the bottom of deep pools, that they congregated and shared the warmest sections of the creek. Now all I had to do was hike, find the fish, and offer my flies. The stream didn't have any deep holes for a while, so I walked up the frigid creek farther into the haze of hardwoods. Sheets of ice encased stones resting in the frigid current. Jagged icicles hung along the edges of small waterfalls like glass teeth, with tiny air bubbles trapped inside each formation.

I walked along the streamside, each step crunching the snow beneath my boots, my footprints filling back in as soon as I took the next step. Soon my footprints would fully disappear, covered by fresh powder, the only signs that I'd been there vanishing as if I had never existed at all. I was a ghost wandering through the valley, all signs of my presence vanishing, the world returning to stillness. About a mile upstream, I found the first pool big enough to hold winter trout.

A wide hole bellied out beneath a five-foot plunge, and rushing water created a hollow hum against the rock wall behind the falls. Whitewater erupted as the current re-entered the stream, foaming bubbles clouding the head of the hole. Swords of ice hung along both sides of the waterfall. The water slowed as it pushed through the hole. The dark, sluggish current poured like wildflower honey wrapping around rocks. The tail of the hole sped up again as the exiting water rose around a freestone shallow.

I stepped through a thin layer of ice along the left bank, the ice crackling beneath the felt soles of my wading boots, and pulled the Biot Midge from the hook keeper of the 2-weight rod. I figured that the fish would be holding beneath the outside edge of foam, the place where the bubbles burst and joined the slick of water. The trout lay in the deepest part of the hole along the oxygen-rich bottom of the pool. I lowered the flies into the water and soaked the midges, the added weight of saturation making them sink faster.

The first false cast was a wide, sloppy loop as I adjusted to the resistance of the strike indicator disrupting the tightness of my cast. The added weight on the leader made it hard to take advantage of the taper. The leader wouldn't roll over, and the green indicator woofed past like a wiffle ball with each progression of line.

My stroke adjusting to the altered rhythm, I finally worked enough line out to hit the head of the hole. The poly-yarn indicator swirled for a moment in the eddy along the right side of the falls and then came down the stretch of water. The green ball of yarn looked like a tangled wad of Spanish moss floating along the middle seam of current. As the indicator reached the back of the hole, I lifted the line from the water and whipped the flies back into the pool, a little more to the right this time.

Fishing in the winter is not like any other time of the year. In spring, summer, and fall, if the fish aren't there, or if I miss a couple of opportunities, then I just wade farther upstream. During warmer months the trout are spread out, each fish finding its own feeding line along the creek. In the winter, however, the fish pod up in the deepest holes holding the warmest temperatures and higher oxygen levels.

In the cold grasp of January, I had to cover every square inch of the pool. I knew of only three or four likely holes in the three-mile stretch of stream I was fishing. With so little good water, I had to make every cast count. It was a one-shot game; either I got my chance or I didn't. Unwilling to waste any energy, trout refuse to budge from their positions in winter water, so missing a single line in a hole might make or break my shot. With every speck of water covered and still no bites, I knew that the fish weren't there, refused to feed, or didn't like my flies. Regardless of the answer, I attached the bottom midge to the hook keeper of my rod, stepped out of the knee-deep current, and walked along the white bank and upstream for the next hole.

What I find in the wilderness gives me the inner strength to face the monotony of modern life. Under the blinding glow of fluorescent lights, I can feel my thoughts race through my mind at warp speed, a frenzy of nonsense slowly driving me mad. I teeter on the edge until I can again stand under the soothing embrace of oak limbs and listen to a mockingbird go through a songbook of impersonations.

I escape the madness of the mechanized world and become in tune, the silence strumming the aeolian harp of my mind. The cold arms of a mountain stream hold me sober, if not forever, at least for a moment.

When I snapped back to reality, the snowfall had slowed until only a few specks fell toward the earth like pieces of confetti hanging on the air before settling amongst the rest. Farther up the creek, the snow stopped completely. The clouds thinned and rose higher around the peaks revealing the afternoon sun, a perfect circle, like an ivory marble hovering above the mountainside without rays or beams or halos. I stopped for a moment and sat down on the back of a limestone boulder, the layer of snow cushioning my buttocks, and stared at the white sun sitting still behind the tangled fingers of tree limbs.

The trees stood like bark-covered skeletons along each slope. I smelled the freshness of the woods, and my breath hung on the cold air. Everything was slowed, and I hesitated to move from that rock, afraid that my movement would break the stillness and shatter the silence. Then the desire to raise a trout smoldered inside me and lifted me from my seat. I continued upstream, headed for the next big pool and the next shot at a finicky fish.

Up ahead, a thick grove of rhododendron hugged the creek. Behind the spearhead leaves, I watched a wide section of water moving between the snow-covered thicket of leaves. I knew the pool well; in fact, that familiar hole was the main reason I chose to fish that section of creek. I walked toward the water, eased through the entanglement of wiry rhododendron, and stepped onto a long slab of granite lining the left side of the stream.

Removing the tiny midge from the hook keeper, I stared into the black surface of the creek. Snow had begun falling again, the soft flakes landing silently on the current and disappearing without a ripple. The pool was at least thirty feet long, and the piece of granite stretched beside the entire hole. A steep trickle entered the silken stream from the right. The deepest section lay along the edge of granite, but the entire pool was five feet at its shallowest, a perfect section of water for winter brookies.

I made my first cast, a short flip into the steady current pushing through the tail. The strike indicator rode high but never bounced across the sheen. I whipped the flies out again, this time closer to the slab of granite on which I stood. Again, the indicator drifted perfectly, but a fish never took. I was beginning to think that my odds of catching a fish were slim, but I wasn't bothered by that reality.

I stripped some line off of the 2-weight and set the cast in motion, this time aiming further into the hole. The flies entered the head of the pool and quickly descended into the unseen. Suddenly the strike indicator sat upright, bobbed a little, and then disappeared under the surface. Unready for the bite, I gathered myself and raised the rod, the slim stick of graphite curving to the water as the fish tugged across the pebbly bottom. The slack line between the reel and the stripping guide shot out of the tip-top as the trout made a run toward the head of the pool. Flashes of yellow and orange lit up the black water as I reeled the fish closer to the surface. With the stiff leader running through the guides of the rod, I pulled the small native from the water and laid the fish on the snowy granite slab.

The flesh of the trout was vibrant against the blank canvas of snow. Snowflakes melted against the skin of the fish as I removed the bottom fly, the Biot Midge, from the trout's hard lip. I took one last look at the brilliant colors of the trout, kissed the fish, and then released the brookie back into the creek. One last spark of yellow flashed as the fish turned toward the dark bottom.

Kneeling on the flat piece of granite, I peered deep into the stream and tried to see the movement of fish, but there was nothing. I laid the rod on the snow and lay back on the rock. Staring up through the crisscrossed lines of overhanging branches, I felt the snowflakes turn to water on my stinging cheeks. I opened my mouth, caught some flakes on my tongue, closed my eyes, and listened to the silence. The slow creak of a shifting conifer rang through the dead air, but I didn't move. I lay still and willed myself to converge with everything.

Glimpses of Monsters

The current eddying around my exposed legs was numbing to say the least. I had no idea that mountain water would be so cold in August, but with my calves burning red I knew that I'd have to buy some waders before too long. I had moved from Charlotte to Appalachia a week before to attend Western Carolina University. I'd packed more rods than socks for my new home, and this was my first attempt casting to mountain trout. The fish were there. I could see them, but a trout had yet to rise.

Since I was a boy I'd loved the coloration of brown trout; and my heart raced at the possibility to hook one, hold it in my hands, and kiss its slimy flesh. Before I came I studied field guides on the trout of North Carolina and found three trout I could hook in Carolinian streams: brook trout, rainbows, and brown trout.

Brookies were the only trout species native to Appalachia, having swum into these waters over ten thousand years ago during the last Ice Age. The 'bows, on the other hand, were an introduced species. They had been brought from western waters and introduced to test the drags of eastern anglers. The browns were also brought into Appalachia. These fish were native to Germany and first introduced in Michigan for the same reason as the 'bows. However they had gotten here, I wouldn't discriminate. I wanted to catch them all.

After casting for a few hours, I left the Tuckasegee River without ever getting a bite. As I walked across the Wayehutta Bridge I could see the fish shifting along the bottom. From twenty feet up I had no way of knowing what species the finning shadows belonged to, but I wanted to mark each one on my list of fish caught. Climbing into my silver Chevy Blazer and driving away from the river, I vowed to catch every type of trout in the stream. I didn't just want any fish though; I wanted a monster from each species, and I'd spend the rest of my college career checking them off the list.

The Brookie

One afternoon during my sophomore year of college, I waded through Cullowhee Creek in search of rising trout. As I moved along the tunnel under a bridge, the passageway was dark. Mud squished around my wading boots as I glared at empty insect casings stuck to the shotcrete walls like dangling artifacts. The remaining daylight shone at the end of the tunnel, and I could see the stream. Water didn't push through the two middle passageways under the bridge. The creek's current was diverted to the right and left tunnels by a sandbar covered with grass in the middle of the creek. Inside the tunnel seemed awfully snaky, but that was probably more mental than scientific, so I walked through. Being cold, damp, and muddy, the narrow tunnel was a much better place for frogs and mosquito larvae than snakes—but it was eerie nonetheless.

Exiting the tunnel, I saw sunlight and noticed raccoon prints embedded in the sand, the footprints pointing back into the tunnel. I was grateful to be where I could see everything and where the things I couldn't see were far enough away not to bother. As I eased out of the tunnel the creek bent to the left, swept across a freestone bed and pooled up before pushing under the bridge. I stood still in the shadow of the bridge and unhooked my fly from the bottom guide of the 5-weight rod. I tugged on the leader, pulling just enough line through the tip-top to make the cast. With one flick of the wrist, the elk-hair wing landed quietly on the surface and began to ride along the rapid. A trout rose to the Stimulator, and in one quick motion, it opened its mouth, took the fly, and turned toward the bottom. I pulled up, felt weight, and brought the fish to hand.

I held a small eleven-inch rainbow in my palm. Its stubby round head thrashed wildly trying to pulsate its body from my grasp. The rainbow's amber eyes looked downward toward the current as I plucked the size 12 Stimulator from its jaw. I opened my hand slightly to see the fish's color: a pale pink lateral line just beginning to show, dark bluish-gray spots mottled over the pink, and dark black specks scattering its olive back. With the dark mottled spots, the 'bow looked like the wild fish in small streams, but all juveniles wear the parr marks. I kissed its snout and released it back into the cool current.

I swung the fly into my hand and held it between my index finger and the cork grip of my rod. Through the overhanging tree limbs I could see the hole that I'd come for: a beautiful feeder stream emptying into a sand-bottom pool. I made my way upstream, felt soles gripping slick rocks as I stepped against the current. The stream was shallow (except for a short, mid-depth run along the right bank), so I stepped quietly, being careful not to send shock waves up the creek that would startle any fish that held there. In range of a fifteen-foot cast, I stayed in position and looked over the hole.

On the right side of the creek, water flushed from a pipe that ran under Highway 107. The current eddied around a fallen log and slowed as it pushed through a deep pool. The trick was to cast toward the pipe and then let the fly swing onto the outside edge of current as it made its way through the hole. I had done this hundreds of times and caught plenty of fish doing so. I was positive I could do it again.

I stripped enough line to make the cast, wiggled the tip to let a little line out and began false casting. A narrow opening between the overhanging branches lining both sides of the creek behind me made it hard for a backcast. I shot line through the gap and placed the fly into the current. The Stimulator landed smoothly on the backside of the pool and began curving with the current.

Instantly fish rose and began slapping at the fly, but I quickly pulled the Stimulator from the water and let it settle on the current behind me. The fish that had risen were a school of warpaint shiners, a species of aggressive baitfish that can sink a dry fly in a matter of casts. The shiners are beautiful in their own right—mirroring barracudas in shape but with bright red lines down their cheeks and only growing to five or six inches—but they were not the fish I was after.

I edged closer to the pool. Being careful not to move too fast, I approached from the right side using the fallen log for cover. I stood on a sandy bank beside the log and peered deep into the incoming current. A shadow lifted from the bottom and ascended slowly and methodically toward the surface. Just before nosing through the current, the fish lowered back into the darkness. A big trout. Possibly twenty inches. My heart began beating hard against my rib cage.

I played out the scenarios in my head: the trout hadn't risen all the way to the surface; the fish was holding tight to the bottom; it hadn't come up fast; and it was BIG. Running through my options, I decided to attach a dropper off the back of my dry fly. I reached into my vest, pulled out my nymph box, and scanned the rows of flies. I decided on a bead-head Pheasant Tail with a strip of flashback running down the wing case. I tied tippet from the bend of the Stimulator and attached the nymph eighteen inches down. Hopefully, the fish would rise.

I cast the flies on the far side of the log, hoping that the barrier would slow the drift. The flies held tight to the bark, and I saw a shadow begin to emerge. The fish came up on the nymph, but in a moment of refusal, sank back to the sandy bottom. I made another cast, but the trout didn't appear again.

Evening glow shone through the limbs of a forty-foot eastern redbud, and crickets began to call from the field grass. I checked my flies and peered back into the sheen. Suddenly I saw the fish fin under the log and swim into the shallow pool of slack water at my feet. The trout was less than two feet from the tip of my left boot, but, surprisingly, was not startled by my presence. The fish was too close for me to make a cast, so I held the rod tip high and tried to drop the flies right over the trout's head. The Pheasant Tail slid down the trout's thick cheek, spooking the fish back under the log. A moment later the trout came back into position, and I tried again.

The Pheasant Tail Nymph dangled from the bend of the Stimulator and hung right above the fish's snout. The trout rose a few inches and, in a short opening of gills, sucked the fly into its mouth. I raised the rod hard, setting the hook into the trout's toothy jaw. The fish tore off downstream, and I let it run, fearing tension might snap the tippet. The line held and, with a few slow reels, the trout was flapping in the shallow water at my feet. With my right arm fully extended, holding the rod high over my head, I bent toward the creek to wrap my free hand around the fish. The strain was too much and the tippet popped. The fish was free. Instinctively, I dove onto the trout's back, straddled its thick body between my thighs, dropped the rod, and grabbed. The fish squirmed but my grip was tight. The trout was mine.

My hand could barely fit around the arched back of the brook trout. The brookie's back was humped like a male salmon's; and he had an upturned kype, the distinctive hooked upper jaw of an adult male trout. I unhooked the small nymph from his kype and laid him on the grassy bank. The fish was a solid nineteen inches and thick in girth. I know he would have been a record brook trout in South Carolina, but here he was no record—although equally a leviathan. His dark lavender back faded into mustard yellow around the stomach, his sides were dotted with buff yellow spots, and his maroon fins along the stomach were tipped in chalk white. I took a quick photo, kissed the fish, and held him in the water, allowing him to slowly tail away into the bottom. He was a monster brook trout, and as he finned away I lay back on the grass and lit a smoke. One down and two to go.

The 'bow

Four days before I graduated with a bachelor's degree in literature, I was headed for water. My education had taught me a lot about "the greats" and literary criticism, but on the streams surrounding the campus, I found myself. Learning from distinguished Chaucerians and Miltonists was fantastic—don't get me wrong—but trout became my professors of life, my piscine colleagues, my reason to wake up and breathe. During my college career I had reeled in a humpbacked nineteen-inch brook trout and a solid eighteen-inch rainbow, both big fish, but I wanted a twenty-incher. More specifically, I wanted a twenty-inch brown that would end my quest.

So Sara and I headed to the Tuckasegee River to try to catch my graduation present. I believed that today the river would bless me with one final gift. We drove to the hole I had nicknamed Beaver Kill Hole after seeing a wounded beaver bludgeoned to death by two rednecks wielding giant sticks trying to end its misery, because I knew there would be an opportunity for big fish. Before my fishing partner, Zac, had graduated and left town, we had consistently brought large trout off the bottom to take flies in that hole. On one memorable afternoon, I caught the eighteen-inch 'bow, and Zac caught a beautiful twenty-two-inch brown trout. The photographs of that day are prized possessions: Zac holding a pancake brown, leopard-spotted giant and me with a gorgeous rainbow sporting a thick red lateral line. The point is, Beaver Kill Hole held big fish and lots of them.

After parking at a nearby apartment complex, Sara and I hiked up an ivy-covered hill and down a dusty farm road. Beaver Kill Hole was nestled fifty feet down a kudzu-smothered ledge dropping down from the right side of the road. Sara and I walked hand in hand but never said a word. I was focused on the fish that I knew were there.

Sara often joined me on the water. We always talked during the entire ride, but muted our conversation when the stream was in sight. She understood why I was there, and she just enjoyed being in the woods. While I spent hours casting to trout, Sara lifted rocks, searched for salamanders, and crawled around the bank. We each had our own reasons for being there and today was no different.

As the road flattened out to water level, we tromped down a steep mud bank and under the branches of a giant mockernut hickory. Four granite boulders lined the current. Sara climbed up the side of the flattest boulder to lie down, and I made my way around the edge of the deep hole. The steep hill barely left a bank to stand on as I hiked around the outside bend at the bottom of the kudzu ledge, but the water was too deep to wade through. A groundhog munching kudzu leaves stared down from the hillside, then waddled into its hole when I got close. Upstream the river shallowed to soft ripples running over a freestone bed. Finally, around the bend, I stepped into calf-high water above the hole and walked into the stream.

Sara was still in sight, her tiny frame outstretched on the giant chunk of granite. I called her name, she turned, and I smiled. I thought it would be one of my last days in the mountains, and I wanted her to see me in my prime. She flipped her hair out of her face and smiled back, the squints around her eyes visible, even at a distance. "Catch me a big one," she called out, her voice echoing off the hillside.

"I'll try." We ended our conversation and soaked in the silence.

A few stoneflies and caddis were on the water, but there was no great hatch to speak of. Water boatmen skittered in the shallows, and small caddisflies dropped to the surface, sporadically laying eggs. I tied on a CDC Caddis pattern that Roger Lowe, a renowned fly tier from nearby Waynesville, had developed for the Tuckasegee caddis hatch. That fly consistently produced in this hole, and I hoped today would be the same. Out of habit rather than necessity, I also tied a Caddis Pupa off the back of the dry. I started fishing the flies on the swing, letting them drift clockwise across the outside edge of the hole. Once the flies straightened out downstream, I stripped them back in two-inch tugs to mimic caddisflies skittering across the surface.

A fish erupted on the flies downstream, and I instantly set the hook. I yelled for Sara to watch while I reeled in the feisty, stocked brook trout. After a short battle, I held the trout firmly in my grasp, removed the fly, and released upstream, trying not to spook the other fish in the hole. I continued to catch trout with the CDC Caddis for the next hour, but not the big fish I had hoped for.

Discouraged, I headed across the river to the inside bank of the bend and began searching through my fly boxes. The tall American beech overhead cast shadows across the stream. Looking out into the river, I noticed something snaking in the current. My first thought was that it was a piece of trash, probably a bag of some sort caught on a rock, tangled synthetic made lifelike by the movement of water; however, upon second glance I could see it was a big trout "holding steady," as Hemingway would put it. I stripped some line off the reel and prepared to make the cast. The branches of beech wouldn't allow for a standard overhead cast, so I side-armed the flies low across the water and watched as they entered the trout's feeding line. The flies moved directly over top of the trout, but the fish didn't move. Even with a few more nice presentations, the trout never rose, so I decided to change flies.

I had seen a big one-inch stonefly on a leaf, so I decided to tie on a size 12 Stimulator to match the natural. I tied on the elk-hair fly and made the cast. Again the imitation drifted directly over the fish, but the trout would not come off the bottom. I feared that the giant trout was spooked and had put down, refusing to feed because of my persistent pressure. With the fish unwilling to move, I decided to try one last presentation.

The sun had already fallen behind the western peaks, and the evening sky glowed cornflower blue. A caddis hatch began to surface and fish resumed feeding in the deep hole downstream, but the fish I had targeted held firm in the shallow riffles just above Beaver Kill Hole. I picked through my fly box and unhooked a size 6 streamer from the foam lining. The streamer, a Gray Ghost, was tied with brilliant orange floss, silver tinsel ribbing, a white wing, and jungle cock cheeks. The fly was a classic pattern dating back a century, but I had never fished it before. I tightened a Uni-Knot on the hook eye and made my first cast.

The streamer hooked across the current and swung around the backside of the trout. Through clear water I watched the huge fish angle on the streambed and then fin back to its holding position. The next cast would have to be shorter in order to swing in front of its nose. I reeled in a couple of feet of line and made the cast. Again, too long, and the fly drifted right across the back of the fish. The trout jolted to the right and then slowly repositioned itself on the seam of current. If it hadn't been spooked before, it was damn sure scared now, but I tried again.

I reeled in a couple more feet and repeated the cast. This time the fly curved right in front of the fish, and as the Gray Ghost was stripped through the water, the trout rose slowly, bit hard, and descended. I set the hook. I wish I could say that the fish bolted downstream tearing line from the reel and taking me to the backing, but surprisingly the trout swam slowly, shaking its head as it was pulled by the rod's tension. In a burst of energy, the trout took off downstream for a brief moment, ripping the line that dangled between the stripping guide and fly reel. I tightened the drag and played the trout toward me, but I had one problem: I wanted a picture taken and Sara was forty yards downstream with the camera. I yelled for Sara to ready the camera as I began making my way downriver toward her. I just kept screaming, "It's BIG! It's BIG!" over and over as if the words needed to be echoed for emphasis.

I saw the fish roll near the surface and instantly knew it was the biggest trout of my life. "This is the biggest trout I've ever caught! This is the biggest trout of my life!" I yelled, restating the same words in every possible form. I walked carefully along the sandy bank curving around the inside edge of the hole. The water was shallow on the side where I stood, but I didn't know how in the hell I could make it to where Sara was.

Looking across to the boulder where Sara sat, I saw a few scattered stones lining the bottom of the river. The stones were just high enough to keep me from swimming and just close enough to be navigated by foot. This was the only shot I had. I kept the line taut and began wading across, carefully stepping on each scattered stone. I had to be sure not to put too much pressure on the fish or else the tippet was sure to snap under the weight, and I had to make each step perfectly so that I wouldn't fall in. Rocking on a stone, I made it there, pulled the fish to hand, and showed off my graduation present.

Pictures show a twenty-three-inch rainbow stretched across my cradled arms. The 'bow's soft pink cheeks seem to blush from the embarrassment of being fooled. A pale cherry blossom pink line runs thinly down the trout's sides. The fish is covered with black specks peppering its olive and silver body. My smile stretches from ear to ear, cheekbones raised high with satisfaction. This is my proudest photograph. That rainbow trout was the biggest trout I'd ever caught—an absolute monster on this river. Since that day, I've caught other trout over twenty inches, but none stands out in comparison. Coming four days before graduation seemed prophetic, a generous gift from the river I'd devoted the past four years to learning.

I left the stream that day in awe. Cicadas buzzed from every limb, and the sky smoldered a lilac purple. I dismissed all thoughts of good grades and graduating cum laude. With the twenty-three-inch fish caught and released, I felt my college career was finally complete. Sara talked to me on the walk back, but I was speechless. My body was stirring with excitement as Sara wrapped her arms around me and kissed me on the cheek. My smile never lowered. I smiled for the rest of the night and into my sleep. That trout was by far the best present I received and was another check on the list. Two down and one to go.

The Brown

While living in Jackson County, I had caught plenty of big trout in the last few years, including the monster brookie and the big 'bow. Now in graduate school, the only thing left on my list was a fat-bellied brown trout. I'd seen friends catch twenty-inch browns with toothy mouths gaping and pitch black spots haloed in crimson. Envy is not a strong enough word for my yearning. I had to catch a big brown. It was a must.

I've always been drawn to fish, and my favorite freshwater species as a kid was always the brown trout. That golden coloration had always seemed fascinatingly unnatural to me. I remember standing in front of the glass at the aquarium in Chattanooga, staring for what seemed like hours at the brown trout holding still in the artificially generated water. I read about their origin, as well as their introduction into North American waters. Amazingly, fly fisherman actually despised the European trout in the beginning, claiming that they were not sporty and refused traditional offerings. Their disapproval meant little to me. I knew that I had to catch a goliath brown.

On the day that I saw the fish of my dreams, I was not even planning on catching a big trout. I entered the water at Webster Bridge, upstream of Beaver Kill Hole, at eight o'clock in the morning. There were thick clouds in the sky, but rain hadn't fallen. I knew the torrents would come: I could smell the heaviness of summer rain in the air and could see it in the upturned leaves. There'd been few showers recently and the water was low, but the clarity was unusually darkened in the dim light. A sparse mayfly hatch carried over from the night before, and dead mayflies floated past with wings like willow leaves. Trout rose slowly, sipping the bugs from the film, and I knew it wouldn't take long to fool a fish.

I reached into the river and scooped up one of the spent mayflies. The body was a light orange-red. Trying to match the hatch, I chose a Sulphur Spinner that I'd tied and never fished. My imitation wasn't an exact match, but maybe close enough to trick a trout. With the fly dangling from 6X tippet with a three-and-a-half-pound breaking strength, I cast into the slow run along the left bank. As the Sulphur drifted across the riffles, a shadow moved from the sandy bottom and, with its nose barely breaking the surface, swallowed my fly. I pulled up, felt the trout swimming toward cover, and turned the fish with steady tension from the 5-weight rod.

With the fish reeled into my grasp, I held a gorgeous fourteen-inch brown trout with a deep ochre back blending into school bus yellow around the belly. The fish was covered from snout to tail with leopard spots, some outlined with red coronas. The trout was breathtakingly beautiful but lacked the size of my dream brown. After kissing the fish on the snout, I went back to casting.

Trout came up all over the water, grabbing mayflies like takeout lunches. I caught fish after fish for hours as I waded downstream.

Surprisingly, every fish all morning was a brown. And to think those fly fishermen who first encountered brown trout in American water said that they wouldn't rise to a dry fly. The Tuckasegee browns certainly were rising during the closing hours of this mayfly hatch, and quite sportingly as well, a hell of a fish to fight on the fly and gorgeous enough to hold me speechless.

Around eleven o'clock, I stood in the deep bend just above Beaver Kill Hole. A light drizzle sprinkled the water's surface, each drop producing liquid fireworks as the ripples spread into convergence. With rain coming down, the trout had stopped rising, losing sight of passing mayflies amid the chaos of undulating droplets pouncing across the top of the water. I searched through fly boxes for a Woolly Bugger, opting to fish a large pattern deep. I found a glittery, chartreuse Bugger with a golden bead head, barred silicone legs, and yellow Flashabou shimmering through the olive tail. Bright, big, and buggy, this fly would be perfect.

The first cast swung along the current and was hammered, producing a nice, stocked brook trout. The next cast ended with the same result: a short fight, a stocked brookie, and a smile on my face. The action held firm, every cast producing a trout, for the entire shower. I caught trout on that fly until the palmered hackle was ripped away from the body, and even then the fish continued to nail the half-naked Bugger.

By the time I reached the top of Beaver Kill Hole, I'd caught and released at least forty fish. I could have ended my trip right then, but I had just made it to the most productive section of river and was certain the Beaver Kill would bring a chance for a big one. Catching big trout is like hitting the lottery. On normal water the chances of catching monster fish have similar odds to winning a million dollars. In Beaver Kill Hole your odds of winning the jackpot increase to scratch-off chances.

The drizzle began again, disrupting the calm pool and sending the fish back to the bottom. It began to rain harder, and I continued to cast the chartreuse Woolly Bugger into the current, allowing the fly to sink as it curved through the deep hole, but the bite had diminished midday. I wanted to wait out the rain, see if I could hook a few more fish, but the trout refused to bite.

Looking downstream, I saw a lone mayfly weathering the storm, its translucent wings pelted by the downpour. In the last bend of river before the current quickened, the mayfly dove to the surface, briefly touching water as it laid eggs. The mayfly's mustard-colored body was encircled by gray from its thrashing wings. As the fly descended toward the surface, a gargantuan brown shot through the sheen, tightening its jaws around the fly as it came through. The huge fish never bent its body and looked like a migrating salmon shooting up a waterfall as it tilted its head back into the current. The fish had to be well over thirty inches.

I had seen the fish as clear as day, dusty brown body and goldenrod stomach, launch through the surface and snack on the bug. I moved downstream to within casting range and started planning my approach. With the first cast following the feeding line perfectly, I was confident I could get a bite, knowing good and well that big trout will often feed during heavy rain. With the Woolly Bugger straightening out, slowly coming to the top downstream, I false cast once and put the fly back in line. Again, nothing. I cast to that fish for four hours, never getting a nip. I tried every fly I could find in my vest, but the trout had disappeared as if only a hallucination.

At three o'clock, with my legs aching from trudging through waist-deep water for seven hours, I headed to the truck, disgusted. Any pleasure the forty trout I'd managed to catch gave me vanished the instant that trout broke the surface. All that remained was the one I had seen. I knew a trout that big would not be likely to migrate from that stretch of water. That fish had probably found a place that offers more than adequate forage and stuck there. Now, I had to find a way to hook it.

I planned the attack. I would go to Beaver Kill Hole at night, bearing a 7-weight rod and some of the biggest flies I could put on my vise. I reread the words of Joe Humphreys, George Harvey, and James Bashline, sucking in every bit of advice they offered on big browns after dark. I tied the flies they mentioned and prepared for battle.

The night that I went a thick green drake hatch hovered over the river. The quarter moon gave enough light to see but—if I were lucky—not enough to spook the fish.

I started off fishing a Whitlock Mouse pattern, hoping that the fish would bust the deer hair off the hook shank. The enormous fly woofed past like a bat as I made casts upstream. Nothing. Suddenly I saw the big brown explode on a landing drake, the splash reflected with dim moonlight. Just as before, I watched the fish come up, feed, and disappear. The giant trout was even keeping the same feeding line. I spent hours that night casting everything I had to no avail. Anthropomorphizing or not, that fish was smart.

Dumbfounded, I hiked toward the truck, the blue beam from my flashlight illuminating the gravel farm road. I had seen the fish again, had been there at perhaps the perfect time, and again nothing. I dream about that monster nightly, often shaken awake by the realization there's one fish left to mark off. I wake up, go there again, cast the line, pray for the bite, and occasionally see the mighty fish rise. I cannot stop because I know it's there. I will not quit because I know it's real. Someday that fish—damn near three feet long—will come to my hand. I will marvel for a moment and release it, but for now, there's still one to go.

Native

A ClackaCraft drift boat bobs down an eddy, and, from the echoing dialects, I can tell that the passengers aren't from North Carolina. The Tuckasegee's mighty flow is foreign to them. I quickly strip in my olive Woolly Bugger and roll cast into slack water that won't possibly be holding fish. Whatever I do, I can't let these bastards know I'm on to a school of big stockers. As the aquatic Cadillac inches closer, I see my fly line straighten out across the surface and instinctively set the hook. After a short fight, I hold a twelve-inch brook trout (obviously of the stocked variety with its piss yellow spots, algae-colored back, and fishier smell) in my hand. I remove the hook, kiss the fish, and watch as the trout fins away into the freestone bottom.

"That was a pretty nice fish," shouted the man stirring the oars in the middle of the boat, obviously the guide.

"Yeah, he was all right."

"You had any luck?"

"Nope. That's the first fish I've caught all day," I state sharply, deliberately avoiding the success I'd had in that hole.

"Well, we've caught a lot of fish on dries," the stocky out-of-towner offers from the rear. The man in the back of the boat looks like some ill-suited mama's boy trying to fit into a world he would die in if left alone. He reminds me of Francis Macomber in the Hemingway story, only sloppier, probably richer, and a tad more northern. This jackass is completely out of his element: a dented Gilligan hat strapped tight around his double chin, a baggy L.L.Bean button-down trying to cover his beer belly, spotless waders obviously bought that morning from the outfitter, white sunscreen spread across his pitted nose like wet bird shit. I noted the beautiful Hardy reel attached to the cork seat of a Scott rod and thought, That rod is far too glorious to sit in his sausage fingers.

"Yeah, we've had some luck on dries upriver. We've caught twenty or so," the guide states as he backpaddles to stay out of my hole.

The client in the front of the boat, who I perceived a mute until now, proudly says in some Bostonian jumble of syllables, "They were all brookies."

"And every one of them were natives," the tubby one claims as he throws a giant loop of line like a lasso for an elephant into a run across stream.

"They were all native?" I ask, confused by the statement.

"Yeah, they had white fins and everything," the once-silent one speaks again. Having heard more than enough, I tell them they can go on through.

The guide begins paddling downstream, and as they disappear behind a line of dogwoods blooming on the bank, I cast and wonder what in the world that guide had told them. The odds of catching native brookies in a river contaminated by farm-bred trout is pretty rare, and it's utterly impossible to catch twenty "all native." As for the white fins, I've yet to catch a brook trout, native or otherwise, that didn't have ivory tips running down their pectorals: it's just a part of their beautiful construction.

My line floats along the current and then curves upstream as another trout is fooled by the Bugger. This fish is bigger and takes off downriver using the current for advantage, ripping drag as he goes. I edge the fish into the shallows and wrap my hand around his broad back. The Woolly Bugger holds firm right in the tip of his rounded snout. The brookie is a good sixteen inches, covered from gill to tail with pale dun spots, and white fins to boot. He *must* be a native.

For me, the word *native* carries a tremendous amount of weight. It is not a word that can be taken lightly, thrown around fly shops like stories of thirty-inch trout, uttered from the lips of people who have no clue what the word really means. For me, those two syllables comprise what has been nearly lost.

I drive through cities where the only trees that grow were planted for ornamentation, rooted into shoveled holes, and encircled with bales of pine straw. The world I live in has become a society that views blooming Bradford pears as street art, not as something that belongs. Few things anymore belong. In all honesty, even I don't belong, but at least I have an eye for what does.

The word *native* defines something that not only is present, but also was; something that has been and should remain; something that bore witness, adapted, and survived. I can understand the desire for something native, the reason why outsiders look to the trout and are proud, but the misuse of such a word is a denial of what we humans have done.

Brook trout, true native brookies—not the ones raised in tanks, shipped in trucks, and dumped in rivers—once filled the cold mountain streams of the Southern Appalachians. Now, the specks that remain are found in places where people are not. They've swum upstream into mountain hollows where the presence of man has not yet encroached, places where hillsides are scattered with moss-backed boulders rather than fading McDonald's cups. The trout that populate most rivers and streams are not part of the place; rather, they're something that has been shipped in, outsiders, just as I am when I wade waist-deep into the river's chilling embrace. There's a reason why fish have to be stocked into rivers that were once the homes of finicky wild trout. There's a reason why the brookies caught in the Tuckasegee River look more like lake trout than like their native brethren. To use the term *native* to describe something that does not belong is to deny that something else been forced out.

Nothing is native about the brown trout and rainbows that fin through Appalachian streams. Some browns and 'bows have become wild in Appalachian waters, but those fish swam into the same creeks and tributaries that the native specks found refuge in, and although I love catching browns and 'bows, I realize those trout are as invasive as starlings, kudzu, and woolly adelgid.

The same is true of most brook trout that are plucked from the current by overweight retirees fumbling through the water like tranquilized bears. Those opaque brookies with faded spots and colors as dull as winter are not the same trout that originally settled in the untainted waters of Southern Appalachian creeks. My love for true native brookies diverts my need to correct outsiders' stories. There still are places untouched where native fish rise to a perfectly played fly, and I think that I'll keep those creeks to myself.

A few weeks into my sophomore year of college, I stood on the bank of Piney Mountain Creek, along the Jackson County border, where I had first caught a native trout. Hickories, oaks, and pines towered overhead. Thick branches of rhododendron and laurel guarded the banks as I stood at the edge of the cool mountain creek. The only sound was the babbling of water as it rippled around and across the smoothed stones and misted the petals of jack-in-the-pulpits. I was ensconced in the wildness of Appalachia.

Stepping into the creek, I felt its cold current wrap around the flesh of my legs. The feeling was awakening, a refreshment for my senses in the warm summer air. I saw an endless line of waterfalls, plunge pool after plunge pool, streaming down the mountainside. I looked into the bubbly foam of the closest pool. It couldn't have been more than two feet in diameter, but I knew there was a fish there. Whipping two flies onto the water, I watched as the dry fly was drawn in a slow circle toward the waterfall. As the size 14 Yellow Sally got to the edge of the foam, the fly shot underwater like a high diver entering the pool from twenty feet above. I lifted my rod and felt the pulsating tension of the trout. The fish had bitten the dropper, a small Hare's Ear Nymph, mimicking a stonefly, dangling from the dry. The trout sensed the pull of my rod and darted downstream, past where I was standing and into the next pool. I stepped into the water below, leaned down to wet my hand, and pulled the brookie toward me. Brought into my palm, the trout's fleshy body squirmed as I lifted him from the water. He was gorgeous.

The brook trout is the only salmonid native to the Southern Appalachians, and over time the southern strand of trout has evolved. Genetics prove that the native Southern Appalachian brook trout differs from other populations of brookies on a subspecies level, and I like to think they are superior to those other strands. Yet, in the small creeks they inhabit, the southern strand of brook trout doesn't grow to be nearly as large as their northern cousins. Down here a twelve-inch speck is considered a trophy.

I held the eight-inch brookie in my hand and marveled at his beauty. His back was emerald green, covered with jade spots placed like puzzle pieces. Along his sides were yellow and blood red dots. His belly was sunflower yellow; his throat, a pure, clean white. The pectoral, pelvic, and anal fins were that blend of red and orange that is only seen during fiery sunsets. The tips of those fins were lined with the same pure white as his throat, a white as pure as cumulus clouds. I was awestruck. Only a native Southern Appalachian brookie would be this well-dressed. I kissed him on his snout and released him downstream, still feeling euphoric as I stepped away.

Continuing up the creek for at least three miles, I climbed up waterfall after waterfall, catching fish after fish. It seemed like all of the plunge pools and even the small, shallow runs held trout. By the time I reached the place where the abandoned logging road crossed the creek, I had caught over thirty brookies. None of them was more than ten inches. Most of them were between six and eight, but all of them wore the same brilliant hues. They were dressed in war paint like native tribes ready to attack. Their sharp greens, yellows, and oranges shot through the water like arrows as they came up, engulfing my flies with an instinctive intensity. Primal.

They were native, as native to these parts as the Cherokee—or maybe more so. As I walked back, I realized just how out of place I was and how perfectly suited to their environment they were. This was their creek, their home—they belonged.

I will rarely share secrets about places that still hold populations of native trout. The reason for this is simple: few places are left. In the past few years, I've watched countless streams (which once provided sanctuary for breeding brookies) be filled with sediment, tainted with runoff, warmed by deforestation. Multi-million dollar estates spring up along mountain brooks like Walmarts. Developers brutally clear-cut mountainsides, grade hills, pave entrance roads, and build mansions. Then when they're all done, they slap a sign at the entrance with a picture of a trout or a fly and a name like "Trout Reserve." The only thing reserved is done so for the highest bidder with no room left for native fish; after all, there are plenty of farms with truckloads of trout at a decent price, and for the millionaires, these are as "native" as they need them to be.

One reason rich retirees escape to the mountains is to enjoy the same qualities they destroy when they come. Driving down a meandering road toward a native stream, I see bulldozers scraping the earth bare, cutting into clay banks, and rolling boulders like marbles. The sputtering smoke from earthmovers conceals the clouds and the mechanical clatter of engines sounds like the fast talk of an auctioneer: "OnedollaronedollaronedollarSOLD to the lovely gentleman in the pinstriped suit." As for me, I drive to one of the few wild places left, try to raise a fish, hold him in my hand, and get one last look while I still can.

In all of my years talking to other fly fishermen, few have shared my passion for native fish as deeply as Ron Rash. He still calls them specks, a word passed to him through thick Appalachian roots (even the title of one of his short stories). Ron's hound dog eyes light up like struck matches when I mention a twelve-inch native brookie; his methodic southern accent speeds to a New York pace, and his limber frame begins to shift from foot to foot. One word describes his posture: excitement.

When Ron asked me if I would take him and his son to a native stream, I couldn't say no. Chances to share my passion with someone who knows and understands my blazing desire are rare. With Ron, I shared two passions: writing and trout. I could tell him about secret streams because as soon as the words were spoken, they were remembered but dead, resonating in his mind and memory alone, never to be spoken of again, taken to the grave.

The May sun was pushing straight down on my shoulders. Ron's wife was pulling weeds in an area crawling with fire ants while he and his son, James, stood by the open door of their minivan. I grabbed my waders, boots, vest, rod tube, and reel from the cab of my pickup. I threw my gear in the van, and we all hopped in: James behind the wheel, me riding shotgun, and Ron in the back.

The music of the Red Hot Chili Peppers came through the speakers; James drummed on the steering wheel as the van curved through mountain roads on the way to my secret stream. Ron was reclined in the backseat, his hands pillowing his head, his long, slender legs straightened and crossed between the front seats. We swapped fishing tales, the stories ricocheting off one another and triggering more: stories of fish caught, fish lost, and fish seen. "Tell him about that carp I caught on the fly rod," Ron urged his son.

"Man, that fish was big. Dad and me were fishing in a pond and he hooked that big ol' sucker. It took him for a ride but he got it in," James explained, words rushing from his lips.

"Yeah, I saw that thing feeding, and I went over there and put my fly in front of him, and he sucked it in," Ron continued in his soft, lackadaisical voice, the words never rushed, only chewed for a while and then coming out effortlessly. "My rod was bowed up pretty good before I got him in. He was about this big..." He held out his arm, and ran his finger across his forearm to where the fish would've ended.

"That thing was big," James finished.

"Yeah, I hooked into a huge carp when I was a kid," I continued the stories without a pause. "That one was about three feet long and around twenty-five pounds. I fought that thing for an hour or so before I ever got it close. Snapped my tippet and was gone."

"Some folks eat them things." Ron rolled the conversation on.

"I know," I replied. "My uncle caught one one time, and a bunch of guys fishing from the bank asked him if they could have it. When he asked them what for, they told him they were going to make carp burgers. Seems like them fish'd be greasy as hell. Pull over right there." I directed James to a carved-out section of gravel, the last parking spot for anything other than off-road vehicles.

We all stopped talking as James pulled to the side of the dirt road and cut the engine, three fishermen itching to get in the water and try our luck. We hopped out in unison and walked to the back. Ron and I started putting on our waders, lacing our boots, and rigging up our fly rods. Ron had his old bamboo rod back now, and, just as I had suspected, the cork was beautiful. James, wearing shorts and sandals, ran monofilament through the guides of a micro-spinning rod. When Ron had told me that his son wasn't a fly fisherman, I instantly thought he couldn't be raising him right. After talking with James, I picked up on his love of the wild and assumed that the lack of fly rod was circumstantial; he just hadn't reached that part of his angling development, and I knew of no better man to get him there than Ron.

With flies cinched tight to tippet, and a chocolate brown Trout Magnet hooked to the eye of James's rod, we headed up an old logging road toward the growing murmur of fast water. The air was cool, even for May, beneath the cover of new growth white oaks, red maples, and shagbark hickories. The dense forest cloaked the smell of conifers, morning glories, and fresh water. We remained silent; the only sounds were chirping wrens, the scatter of squirrels across dried leaves, and the creek. We could have continued the conversation, but what can be said in a place so magnificent? The wild had left us speechless.

The stream was right beside the trail now, the cold current pushing under low branches of rhododendron, then dropping into open pools as it ran through the valley. We got to a place where the land flattened out beside the stream, shallow runs working through a mountain hollow, a steep bank all that separated us from the current. "This is where I usually get in," I said. Holding to the thin trunk of a redbud, I eased down the bank, scattered with Dutchman's breeches. Layers of wildflowers and underbrush covered the flat, but we were all focused on the stream, all of us staying far enough back not to spook any fish hiding just beneath the ripples. "Go ahead, Ron. There's usually a fish holding right there in the middle where the current wraps around that rock." I pointed toward the stream with my rod tip.

"James, you go ahead." Ron passed the torch.

"No, you get in there and show me how it's done." James refused the offer, choosing to see his dad catch the first fish. Ron didn't pass up the chance again. As he crept toward the moving sheen, he pulled his fly, a weighted Woolly Worm (his go-to fly for every situation) from the stripping guide and took out just enough line from the reel to make the cast. He worked the backcast beneath leaf-strung branches and dropped the fly just above the ripple. An orange strike indicator ran along the seam as the Woolly Worm bounced along the freestone bottom. James and I watched closely. Staring at Ron, I could sense the emotion of a man who had finally come home, a man who knew nothing better than mountains, cold streams, and native specks. He set the hook as the Woolly Worm passed through the section I knew kept fish.

"Missed one." Ron turned toward us. James and I remained transfixed in meditation. I saw the perfect convergence of man and water. I never questioned whether or not Ron fit; the answer was obvious as his leggy frame and scruffy shave melted into the thin trunks and rough bark of red bays. After a few more casts, Ron gave the next section to me. He hadn't hooked a fish, but he had missed one, a sure sign that trout were there.

I began throwing flies to incoming seams of current. The Parachute Adams rode flat upon the run, the dangling Pheasant Tail dragging across stones as the flies came back toward me. A trickle along the left bank emptied into a small pool, bubbled, and rejoined the brook. I knew there would be a fish keeping steady on the sandy slope of the pool. Whipped into the trickle, the Parachute Adams disappeared into the bubbling foam, emerged on the inside cut, and curved toward the main current. The Adams, yanked under with force, vanished. I set the hook and felt fish, the 2-weight rod pulsing. I lifted a small native from the stream—its colors a squirming reflection of a James Prosek painting—and held the speck out toward Ron and James.

"Look at that, James. That's a speck. That's the fish I write about." Ron explained the magnificence to his son, who had not yet caught a wild trout. James peered hard at the glorious marmorations of the brook trout, the fire orange fins and gut. If a picture's worth a thousand words, a brookie's worth a million. Yet, there was nothing to say, all of us awestruck. Lowering the trout back into the stream, I watched the fish merge back into the darkness and vanish among the rounded backs of stones.

James took the next stretch. He was larger than his father but just as agile in the stream. Tossing the small lure, he had a hard time keeping up with the quickness of a narrow rush of water. When he reeled too slowly he got slack line, too fast and the presentation was unnatural. I sensed that if Ron and I couldn't push James to pick up a fly rod, this outing might. James got a couple of bites but was unable to set the hook.

Ron took the lead and sidearm cast under overhanging branches that enclosed the stream in a tunnel of foliage. His touch was soft, the placement perfect. The fluorescent orange strike indicator disappeared, Ron pulled up, and a fish was on. With fish in hand, Ron stared into the trout's red jasper eyes, took in every speck of splendor, and released the fish back into the water.

We took turns as we headed upstream, rotated positions to give everyone a shot at trout. Ron and I generally hooked into something or at least got bit on our turns, but James was having trouble adjusting to the small scale of a native stream, where everything must be perfect. I could see that James was getting antsy, itching for a speck of his own. A large, deep hole widened at a place where lichen-covered boulders worked as dams along the banks. If there was a place for James to hook a brookie, this was it. The water was deep and wide, a perfect spot for his lead-headed Trout Magnet. He cast the dark brown grub into the current and held the rod high, keeping the lure down, but not sunk. The line twitched, the rod wavered, and he set the hook without hesitation.

James's eyes lit up with the same passion I'd seen in his father. Until that point, I hadn't thought James looked very much like his father. Ron was tall and slim, lanky like me, and James was mid-height and stocky like a football player. Yet, in that excitement, I saw the same glint flare from his pupils, the passion for things wild, a bond perhaps deeper than blood. "I got one!" James called to make sure his father took notice.

As Ron walked across a pebbly shoal toward his kneeling son, I was reminded of fishing with my dad, unforgettable moments shared on the water, James held the beautiful native proudly in his hands, carefully removing the hook, holding the fish just long enough, and releasing the trout back into the unknown.

With slime still fresh on his palms, James looked up at Ron with an unbreakable smile. In that instant two words seemed to pass between them: "I understand." Maybe I've romanticized the moment, dramatized an innocent smile, but I witnessed something, one more thing shared between father and son: a fish that belonged, an acknowledgement of what it meant to be wild and native, the life force of Appalachia.

James and I continued up the stream, swapping holes, the one in back always looking on at the one in front, both wanting to see a fish. After a while, I noticed that Ron was no longer with us. I turned around and saw him about thirty yards downstream. He was sprawled out across the cool surface of a flat granite car-size boulder covered with lime green lichens like fungal camouflage. Through leaves spread like hands across a glass pane, he stared up into the afternoon sky. He adjusted his legs, shifted his spine, and closed his eyes. Only one thing can fuse a man to a place like this—only one thing, and all three of us knew exactly what it was.

The Ritual

When a fellow graduate student mentioned he wanted to learn how to fly fish, I immediately offered to take him. I rarely invited anyone to join me on the water since Zac had graduated and left Cullowhee, but Greg was different. The courses we had together gave me a slight insight into his priorities and high on the list was his affinity for the natural world. His love for the wild emerged in his writing and his extensive knowledge of the environment was an equal offering to what I could teach him.

He was a man of few words, but when he did choose to speak, it was generally something substantial, borderline brilliant. His short, no bullshit style of speaking reminded me of reading Hemingway's dialogue. I respected him as a writer, a thinker, a lover of the wild; but more importantly, as a man. Time on the water would allow me to get to know him; or if he never opened up, at least there'd be fish.

I loaded the rods into the truck and drove the half mile to where he lived in Cullowhee. I didn't have a clue what to expect when I arrived, but as I pulled into the parking lot behind the small apartment building, Greg was digging through the floorboard of his small pickup. As I parked beside him, he looked up from whatever he was doing and gave me a nod, not much else, little expression.

I got out of the car, lit a cigarette, and walked over beside his truck. Greg looked up, pulled a white undershirt on over his muscular torso, looked at me through thin-framed glasses, and headed toward an open apartment door. I took a drag off the cigarette and followed him to the step. "You can come in," he said, and motioned for me to step into the cluttered apartment. I hesitated, not knowing whether or not I could smoke inside.

"I'm going to finish this cigarette right fast." A small strawberry plant, with a single berry ripened and bright, grew in a terracotta pot outside the door. Beside that, a three-foot tomato vine was tied off to a stick he'd stuck in a larger pot; a few small tomatoes shone green along the stalk. "Where'd you get these plants?"

"I planted those a while back. Ain't producing much." Greg's Georgia accent carried as he walked around the apartment.

"That strawberry looks pretty nice."

"Yeah, there were three, but two of them disappeared. The guy that lives down there on the end said something about them one day, and the next thing I knew they were gone. I bet that son of a bitch ate them." I smirked at his resentment, tossed the cigarette out into the driveway, and stepped inside the small apartment. Two raccoon skins were draped across the back of the couch to the left, and another lay next to a sun-dried tortoise shell on a bookshelf to the right. On a small shelf built on the end of the kitchen counter, a few mason jars held some type of dried plants.

"Where'd you get these hides?"

"A friend of mine sends them to me. He catches them in traps and skins them."

"What's that in the jar over there?"

"Some plants I dried to make tea." From a distance it looked like a Mason jar full of pot, a sight I'd grown accustomed to in Appalachia. Dried plants for tea made more sense. He was big into self-sufficiency and living off the land, but I'd just as soon not take a taste. "You ready?" Greg grabbed a pair of sandals and stood in front of me.

"Yeah. You got everything?"

"Yeah." His olive-colored cargos were rolled up his legs like depictions of Huck Finn, and his T-shirt pressed tight to his back as he walked barefoot across the pavement. As we got into my truck, I remarked to Greg that he hadn't locked the door.

"It's okay. Jen's coming back."

"Who's Jen?" I cranked the engine and began to back out.

"My wife." In the year and a half that I'd known Greg, he never once alluded to being married. I'd noticed a unique band on his ring finger a couple of times, something I later found out she'd made him, but never thought anything of it. Generally, I can tell when folks are married, or at least they'll offer a hint, but Greg never said a word, a testament to how little information he released about himself.

We headed down the road, past some Christmas trees growing on a small farm up a hillside. The midday sun was bright overhead, but the heat would have little effect where we were going.

"Where we going?" Greg asked.

"Mull Creek up at the top of Caney Fork."

"There many fish?"

"Yeah, there's a lot of native trout up there and some pretty nice wild rainbows too."

"Think we'll catch anything?" His succinct questions continued.

"Oh yeah. And you're going to have to kiss the first one."

"Why?"

"Ritual."

Kissing fish had been a habit of mine for as long as I could remember. I first picked it up as a kid after watching Jimmy Houston, the host of a Saturday fishing show on ESPN, kiss every bass he hooked into. As a child whose heroes were all fishing hosts, it wasn't long before I made it a ritual.

I can remember the slimy remnants of bluegills drying on my lips, the pungent smell of fish sticking there after a long day of catching sunfish. The stench brought new meaning to the comeback "It's probably your upper lip." My feeling was that if the pros did it, then it had to be right. So I puckered up. Zac also kissed them. The first time we'd ever fished together he'd made me kiss my first native trout. He didn't know kissing fish was something I would have done anyway. Now, it was my turn to pass on the tradition.

I drove toward the creek, and as we pushed on, Greg began to open up more. We talked about our favorite authors and the art of writing. We joked about the suck-ups in our writing workshops, the ones we both hated, the writers who used the class as a counseling session, and the girl who thought she was the next Emily Dickinson. Greg laughed heartily as I cracked jokes with my usual brutal honesty and disregard for human emotion and, for the first time, I began to see who he was. He wasn't shy a bit; instead, he was completely full of conversation, his strong, silent front just an attribute of his unfettered masculinity.

Before long we were there. The gravel road ended in a small circle where Beechflat Creek joined Mull.

"This it?" Greg asked.

"Yeah, Mull Creek's the one on the left. We're fishing it." As we stepped out of the truck, I grabbed my waders and boots from behind the seat, lowered the tailgate of the truck, and began putting on my gear. "I've got an extra pair of waders in the truck, if you want to wear them, but they might be a little big." I was a good bit taller than Greg, but I had to at least offer.

"I'll be fine." He'd already begun strapping his Teva sandals on.

"You going to be all right wading in those? Might be slippery."

"I'll be fine. This is what I wore when I used to raft guide for the NOC." (The NOC is an acronym for the Nantahala Outdoor Company, a nearby guiding group that takes tourists through whitewater. The Nantahala Gorge offered some nice rapids and often the poorly prepared out-of-towners swam.)

I started rigging up the rods, running line through the guides, and attaching tippet to the end of both leaders. Greg watched intently, learning the knots without ever saying a word. When I began to choose the flies, he asked questions, wanting to know every detail about the entomological basis of each pattern. I explained the dries and nymphs and showed him what we were using. I put a Parachute Adams onto the end of his tippet and dropped a Pheasant Tail sixteen inches off of the bend. For me, I chose a size 18 Stimulator I'd tied to mimic the black caddis hatch and put a dropper identical to his off the back of mine. I handed him his rod, threw the fly vest over my shoulders, and tromped toward the creek.

Greg stopped along the bank, bent down, and looked intently at something growing amidst the dangling ferns. I looked over his shoulder. "Jack-in-the-pulpit." I identified the wildflower as he ran his finger against the bud.

"Yeah, I know. You know a lot about wildflowers?" Greg asked.

"No, not really, but that's my favorite." I'd first been introduced to that particular flower while reading a Silas House novel. It instantly became my favorite for its name and aesthetics. Then a Georgia O'Keefe painting of the flower sealed the deal. I figured Greg knew a lot about them. Hell, he could've probably named every species along the creek, but he didn't continue the conversation.

I pointed to the creek with my rod and began explaining the intricacies of reading water before we stepped close enough to spook any fish. He caught on quickly, his rafting experience giving him a wonderful point of reference, and we moved into the current. A small pool gathered right before the creek separated into two seams. I'd caught a fish there before and used the opportunity to show Greg the technique of dappling native trout from a narrow stream.

Before the cast, I explained the motion and what to do if a trout rose or the dry fly disappeared. In one flip the tiny Stimulator floated on the left seam of the main flow, the elk-hair wing holding the body of the fly in just the perfect angle beneath the surface. I concentrated on the pepper color of the grizzly hackle wrapped around the head of the dry. The gray feather was the only detail keeping the fly visible. Then it was gone and I lifted the rod. A small trout dug into the bubbling head of the pool, but I lifted it through the foam and swung the small native into my hand. We both stared at the seven-inch brook trout, dull with the colors of spring, but still more gorgeous than any fish swimming downstream.

"Pretty, ain't it?" I asked as I held the fish out toward Greg.

"Yeah," Greg agreed.

I kissed the fish and released it back into the pool.

"Now why'd you say you've got to kiss them?"

"Out of respect," I answered as the juvenile speck finned away from my fingertips. For the first time, I realized that the ritual had become more than just mimicry of childhood heroes. It had become a symbol of my undying affection for fish. Until Greg had questioned me, I'd never really thought that deeply about why I did it, but as we made our way up the creek, it began to make sense.

In the fly fishing documentary *Patagonia*, a dialogue breaks out between two fishermen after one of them has just kissed and released a gorgeous Tierra del Fuego rainbow. "You're going to catch some kind of fish herpes, if you keep kissing fish like that," one fisherman says to the other.

"It's a family tradition," the other man replies.

After laughing at the idea of fish STDs, I thought about that brief conversation and about what kissing fish meant to me. I realized, that at some point, it had become more than just habit or tradition. Kissing fish had become more intimate than that.

Looking back, I think I can pinpoint the change to the moment Zac made me kiss my first native trout. When I held that beautiful brook trout, something inside of me evolved. That trout wasn't just another fish on the totem—it was an animal whose heritage had survived here for millennia. That fish was one of the few things unchanged by time and the inevitable influence of man. Now when I hold a trout, especially the first of the season, I take in every speck of color and am careful not to hold it too long. After I've marveled at its beauty, I kneel down and kiss the fish out of respect for what it is, and then I release it back into its world. I'm blessed to share a moment with something so magnificent, and that little peck on the nose has become my way of saying thank you.

The father of my ritual, Jimmy Houston, was asked in a *New York Times* interview whether he had ever kissed any of the fish that he later cooked. His response was simply, "If you was to kiss a fish, put it in the livewell and take it home and eat it—well, that would be like cheating on your wife." I tend to agree. At this point in my life, I've kissed more fish than I have women, and being with the woman I plan to marry, I doubt that will ever change. The ritual has transcended its humble beginnings. The ritual reiterates respect.

As we moved further up the stream, I held back a limb of rhododendron that overhung the creek so that the bent branch wouldn't slap Greg in the face. He'd yet to make a first cast, but I could see in his eye that he was picking his seam. Greg pointed and began to ask, but I just nodded. I stayed back as he crept toward a nice run. He made his cast, the flick of the wrist off just enough to make the fly miss its mark. Greg tried again, and this time the fly landed closer but caught the current and quickly shot downstream. He lifted the fly from the water and rolled the line straight over; the 5-weight rod was parallel to the stream as he straightened his arm and dropped the Parachute Adams onto the inside.

A small native appeared from beneath the ripples, rose to the dry, and took the offering back to its lair. Greg lifted the rod, a delayed reaction, and the fly came back through the surface with no sign of a fish. I almost explained he'd been a little late, that he should raise the rod as soon as the fish rolls over the fly, but his eagerness to recast made it obvious that he recognized his mistake. He dropped the fly directly into the same seam, but nothing stirred. The fish had been spooked and we moved on.

I decided not to cast again until Greg hooked into a fish, so I stayed behind, let Greg take point up the creek, and watched as he maneuvered toward his next pocket. A small eddy circled around the left side of a large piece of quartz. The white stone had a hazy yellow hue where it came out of the water, and a mix of dirt and tiny mossy patches darkened the top of the rock. He didn't point this time, sure of his line, no need to ask for my approval.

Greg dropped the Adams right into the center of the swirling eddy, and as the dry fly circled, a fish rolled on the bottom and sucked in the submerged nymph. The Adams shot underwater and Greg lifted the rod. He had hooked his first true native trout, a landmark in all fly-fishing careers and a huge feat for his first time holding a fly rod. I had taken Greg to that creek because I knew he'd have a lot of chances to hook fish, but hooking up on his second bite boggled me. Needless to say, he took to the game quickly. Greg brought the fish toward him, knelt on the rocky bank, wet his hand as I'd told him, and grabbed the native brook trout. He unhooked the Appalachian marvel and held the gorgeous fish stretched out across his palm.

"That's a damn nice fish!" I said proudly. Greg didn't respond but eyed the beautiful native from tip to tail. This trout was more colorful than my earlier catch, the pectoral fins as red as fall maple leaves. Without my saying a word, he lifted the fish to his lips, his tight pucker as timid as a young boy's, and pecked the native on its nose. Then he lowered the fish to the current and let it dart back toward the standing quartz. He didn't say anything afterward, but his silence meant one thing to me: he understood.

Greg and I took to the water many times after that day, and I never once saw him drop a fish into the stream without first offering a kiss. We became good friends, swapping tales, sharing experiences about the natural world, and growing into men on the water. When I found out Jen was pregnant with their first child, my question was easy: "Is it a boy?" His answer promised one thing—another generation of fishermen. Not to say that a girl couldn't have meant the same, but these things are generally easier to push onto boys.

Greg left the mountains and the trout behind soon after Rowan was born. He found a job teaching at Elon University in the North Carolina Piedmont, but I knew of a few good rivers around that part of the state. All I hoped was that one day he would pass on the ritual. I hoped he'd take Rowan to the water, teach him to cast a rod, hook a fish, respect things wild, and kiss trout.

When Rowan was six months old, Greg and Jen came to visit me. While Greg sat holding Rowan in his arms, he told me about catching a six-pound largemouth bass in Texas the month before. I looked at Rowan's smiling face and then deep into his curious eyes, the same deep brown as his father's. The baby's hands clenched and opened—yearning for a rod, I imagined—and I had no doubt that the ritual would continue.

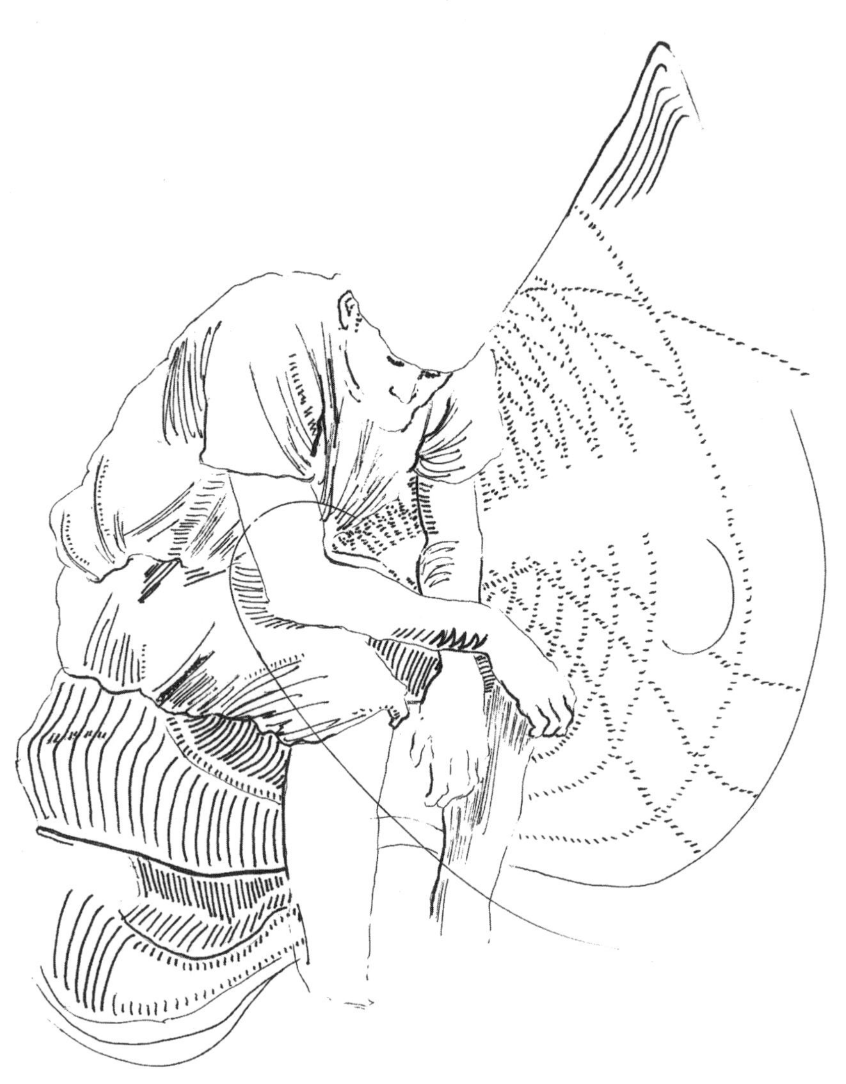

The Grass Eater

Waist-high field grass, overgrown since the cows had been rotated into another pasture, surrounded Johnston Pond. I rarely made it through the thicket without coming out covered in ticks. The shiny arachnids freckled my bare skin like spots on a spaniel; but they rarely got the chance to dig in, feed, and fatten. I was always sure to get them all off immediately when I went home to avoid maternal warnings of Lyme Disease and Rocky Mountain Spotted Fever. Ticks tangled themselves in the hairs of my legs every day, but with a pond full of fish, the reward always outweighed the risk.

For my best friend, Darryl, and me, summer vacation meant one thing—fishing. Every morning the cardinals and chickadees, chirping toward the fiery light growing behind the wooded horizon, marked the time to grab a rod. Like clockwork, I rose out of bed, threw on tattered clothes, snatched up a rod, and headed out the door.

A red clay path meandered through a thick grove of oaks and hickories toward the pond. The hike produced a sensory overload: honeysuckle wafting on currents of fog, bumblebees weaving through wildflowers, bluebirds ruffling feathers drenched with morning moisture, my feet crushing fallen muscadines half-eaten by coons the night before. Smells mingled, colors blended, and calls and sounds mixed accompaniment. Synesthesia.

The clay path ended at a rusted barbed-wire fence lining a cow pasture. The splintered fence posts shifted in the dirt and the brittle wires wobbled under my weight as I crossed and dropped into the field grass. The field grass thinned under the shade of water oaks, and the ground, worn bare by heavy hooves, was veined with thick roots and fallen limbs. Once I walked into the shade, the pond came into view, the fog still hovering tightly above the stagnant surface.

Some mornings Canada geese cut Vs across the pond as they glided like sailboats across the water. Some mornings a great blue heron waded through cattails and pecked minnows from the shallows with its piercing beak. Some mornings chimney swifts sliced air in acrobatic flips just above the surface as they chased one another in avian dogfights. Some mornings a largemouth bass would erupt on a bullfrog kicking across the surface for land. But every morning, I was there, rod in hand, casting for fish, and praying for the big one.

If Darryl wasn't standing on the bank when I arrived, I knew that he would come within an hour. Then, the rest of the day, we would cut jokes from opposite banks, show off our catches, yell our interpretations of the ones that got away, and go home satisfied. At twelve years old, there was nothing else. Fishing was life.

In many ways the fish that get away are more satisfying than the twenty-inch trout that occasionally take the fly. The ones that never make it fully to hand show themselves like frightened ghosts, only for an instant and then are gone. They are fading glimpses, so brief that I often wonder if what I have seen even existed. I feel the pull, see the shimmering body flash in the dark water, smell the flesh as the tail slaps the surface, and then nothing. These are the fish that grow twelve inches by the time the story is told, the fish that lead to tales of Volkswagen-size catfish swimming below a dam, the fish that rip drag, break rods, shatter egos, and never look back. These fish are the reason that I trim my line, tie on a new hook, and cast again.

Few bodies of water have had a line break their surface without stories of a fish of mythic proportion finning through the darkness. For Ahab, it was the white whale. For the characters in *Grumpy Old Men II*, it was Catfish Hunter. For me, in Johnston Pond, it was the grass eater.

I can't remember the first time I saw that fish, but I do remember that originally there were two grass carp chomping algae along the swampy bank. Both carp had been plopped into the pond to try to take care of the encroaching vegetation springing from hot days, stagnant water, and manure-rich mud. The fish certainly did their job, trimming the hydrilla like piscine weed whackers, and I watched, mesmerized by the sheer size of those monsters. Eventually one of them must have died because they no longer swam together. The carp that was left moved just below the surface like a shallow running submarine. From a distance the fish was a dark spot creeping around the pond and staying just high enough in the water column to remain visible—up close was another story.

When I was stealthy enough to move through the field grass and get close to where the fish was feeding, I was able to see every detail of the carp's huge body: the gray snout protruding through the surface; its fat lips sucking in weeds like an infant mouthing a pacifier; its bulging eyes the size of doorknobs; the fanning pectoral fins sweeping the stagnant water; scales as big as fifty-cent pieces rowed down the thick sides making fishnet lines across the golden body; its waving tail unsettling the bottom and creating clouds of mud that darkened the water. As soon as the carp saw me, the water would explode as the fish pivoted and disappeared into the murk.

I stood on the banks of Johnston Pond and scanned the still water every day for that fish. On hot summer days I saw its feeding lips spread ripples as the carp slurped algae from lily pads. In the fall I watched its thick silhouette slowly slide under red, yellow, and orange leaves, flames floating across the sea green surface. Early on cold winter mornings I saw the giant carp feeding on the stalks of dead watergrass under a paper-thin layer of ice. Year round I stared at the carp moving slowly through the shallow pond, and I knew that it was unmistakably the master of its domain. Whereas every other fish swimming in Johnston Pond was forced to stay alert to predators (minnows dodging herons and bream, bream darting from turtles and bass, bass running from other bass and me), the carp had no predator. The fish was three feet long and easily weighed twenty-five pounds. The carp was a tank in a battlefield of foot soldiers, king by sheer size, legendary, and I wanted to hook it.

I don't know of any instance that can destroy a fisherman's vocabulary faster, instantly reverting him to monosyllabic cursing, than when he watches a trophy fish break free and disappear into the darkness. Those moments, more crushing than finding out that Santa Claus isn't real, flip emotions in a heartbeat. Riding an adrenal high, the fisherman stares down at the monster fish slowly coming closer to the net, the fisherman's intense yearning working like psychic control to draw the object closer and closer. Then in one quick snap, all is lost, hearts drop into stomachs, posture melts into a puddle of wax, and all that is left are archaic words like *Fuck! Shit! Bitch! Damn! Ass!* and *Hell!*—often turned into one continual exclamation.

In spite of that, I live for these moments. The single thing that holds me waist-deep in rushing water and casting chicken feathers at invisible trout are the ones that got away. If every fish were landed, I wouldn't have reason to go back. Perfection means an end has been reached and that nothing can possibly be bettered. The firecracker pop of tippet is an instant reminder that while I am good and always getting better, no matter what I do, I'll never be perfect, and the fish will swim on.

Stalks of cattail swayed over Darryl's head like Maduro cigars leaning back and forth in the wind. He was trying to cast a balsa wood Bass Popper along the edge of a lily pad bed, but most of the time the hook ripped into the birch leaves on the backcast. I watched as he sneaked a cast through a break in the vegetation and shot the massive fly onto the surface. With each strip, the sound of the popper, similar to a small pebble dropped into a glass of water, resonated across the pond and the silicon legs pushed ripples like the steps of a water strider.

I'd known Darryl since kindergarten, when he moved onto the only other street in my neighborhood. His folks were both from New York, but he adopted the southern dialect pretty quickly. He was shorter than I, with small, toned muscles. We'd fished every speck of water around our homes, but Johnston Pond was our hideaway where in summertime we'd sneak warm beers and stolen cigarettes to the pond to enjoy brief glimpses of "adult" life between casts.

That day in June, I heard a fish slash out from across the pond toward the popper, saw Darryl set the hook, and watched as he reeled in a hand-size bluegill. The bluegill was a nice fish, a decent fight on a limber fly rod, but we knew bigger fish moved under the algae.

I stood under the branches of a thick white oak, a bent NO TRESPASSING sign scattered with buckshot nailed into the bark. I tied on a Black Gnat with silver tinsel ribbing the body. By the time I cinched the knot, Darryl was reeling in another fish. This time a thirteen-inch largemouth was tearing through the water and slinging tangled hydrilla off the leader.

I grabbed my line three or four inches above the dangling fly and held the Black Gnat under water. The dubbing and hackle soaked up pond water, which made the fly sink faster on the first cast. I flipped the fly into the corner of the pond, a spot shaded constantly by the white oak, and watched as the Black Gnat slowly descended beside a sunken tree stump. A dark silhouette rose through the hazy green water. The sinking fly converged with the silhouette, the floating line pulsed forward, and a fish was hooked.

I didn't have enough line out for a fight, so I raised the rod to lift a small green sunfish out of the water and into my hand. The fish's olive back was a mirror image of the pond's foggy water. A blackened orange colored the fish's belly, exactly the same shade as the sunlight being filtered through the water. The sun, over 96,000,000 miles from earth, appeared on the fish's belly. The green sunfish had been perfectly camouflaged in Johnston Pond, and I wondered if the pigments would change if the fish were suddenly dropped into another body of water. I unhooked the wet fly from the jaw and plopped the fish back in the water. Bream were bedding beside the sunken tree stump, so I knew it wouldn't be long before another one snatched up my fly.

I flipped another cast and readied myself as the Gnat slowly fell into the darkness. Nothing bit. I tried again. Nothing bit, and I soon figured that a snapping turtle had probably come into the shallows and spooked the bedding bream. Instead of moving to another spot, I flicked the fly once more into the pond. A huge outline came up from the bottom like a sunken log finally freed from sediment. The dark silhouette was the grass carp and it was eying the Black Gnat!

As the carp opened its gills, it sucked the fly into its mouth and I yanked. The carp, startled by the prick and onset of tension, took off toward the middle of the pond and ripped drag off the Medalist reel. The trophy I had been after for so long was on the line! All that was left was to play it smart, let the fish run, and slowly tire the beast.

With a giant fish on the line, the instinct is always the same—get the bastard to hand as quickly as possible. There's one problem with this plan—big fish will exploit the smallest flaw in equipment: tight drag, a nick in the line, a loose knot, a brittle hook. In order to hook and land big fish, every detail must be played to perfection.

When patience and fishing are associated, generally patience refers to waiting for a fish to bite; however, the patience it takes to wait for a fish is incomparable to what it takes to land big ones. If the fish wants to run, then it has to be allowed to run. Sometimes I've gained ten yards of line only to have a trout tear off thirty yards on a run downstream. Two steps forward, three steps back. Being unwilling to slowly wear a fish down almost always leads to a freed fish. In time, I've learned not to muscle a fish, to let the fish do what it does, and to rely on my equipment to slowly tire the fish out. If a big fish wants to run, I let it run. If a big fish wants to swim straight at me, I strip in line as fast as I can to keep up. If a big fish tries to swim toward thick cover, I turn the rod and try to pressure the fish into swimming in another direction. What I try not to do is horse a fish in, but that's not to say I've always been this composed.

"Darryl! I got him!" I yelled across the still, green water, my voice echoing off the softwoods surrounding the pond.

"Got what?"

"I got him! I've got the carp!"

Darryl wound in his line stretched out on top of the water, the olive green floating line disappearing from the surface and back onto his battered reel. He tried to come quickly, but he was standing in thick, boggy mud as black as wet coal, making each step a battle just to pull his shoes through the muck. He wove through the cattails and onto the leafy bank with one shoe still on and a muddy sock on the other foot. He had lost a sneaker in the dense mud, but, regardless, he was on his way across the log bridge and around the pond.

"Be easy on him. Don't horse him. Be easy on him," Darryl yelled as he finally got to where I was standing. I couldn't speak because I was paying so much attention to fighting the fish. The carp moved across the pond and swam toward a tiny island covered with field grass and one blooming dogwood that scattered pink petals across the surface as a subtle wind blew from the south. Knowing if the carp made it around the island it would most likely break free, I turned the rod low in the opposite direction of the fish's path to try to pressure it away, but the attempt was useless. The fish moved steadily, pulling line off the reel, quickly inching toward the backing.

As the fish curved around the far edge of the island, I was sure I would lose it, so I let off the pressure and allowed the carp to swim freely. Unexpectedly, the fish turned and moved back around the island into open water. I put pressure on the carp, reeled the monster toward me, and sidestepped to an opening on the bank where there wasn't any grass lining the water. The shallow opening was dense with gray mud, worn bare by hooves and weight as the cows had entered the pond to cool off from the hot summer sun. I thought that I would have a better chance of beaching the carp than reeling it to a steep bank and having to lift it. Assuming I ever got the carp close, I knew the gradual rise to the bank could provide a perfect place to beach the beast.

The monster moved closer as I continued to reel it toward the bank. The carp was within twenty feet, but at any moment the fish might spook and tear off line. I reeled the carp closer and closer, and the leader came into sight. I back-stepped up the bank, my movement altering my reflection on the surface of the pond, the change startling the carp. The fish took off for deeper water, with each stroke of its tail ripping line off the reel.

"You almost had him," Darryl said, standing over my shoulder, watching my every move.

"If I get him close again, get in the water and grab him."

"All right."

The carp was sharking back and forth across the middle of the pond. I began lightly reeling in again, trying to inch the big fish closer. Slowly but surely, the carp came toward the bank. Darryl started moving closer to the water and prepared to wrap his arms around the scaly body of the carp. The fish was nearing range and again the leader became visible, but the fish still swam too deep to be seen.

Darryl took off his remaining shoe and both socks and tiptoed through the clay toward the shallow water. The gray mud squished between his toes as he entered the pond. His footsteps brought bubbles and a cloud of sediment to the surface. Darryl bent his knees, lowering his body toward the clouded water. With dirty khakis rolled up his calves, he stretched his arms over the surface and prepared to grab the fish. The carp came within reach and Darryl shot toward it. With the first sign of movement, the carp thrashed in the shallow water, the drag screaming as the fish pulled back into the deep. Darryl's white undershirt was splattered with muddy water, and he wiped the splash from his face with his forearm.

"Almost." I tried to encourage him, hoping he wouldn't give up.

"As soon as that bastard saw me, he was gone. That fish is spooky as hell."

"Yeah, but we'll just keep working him in till he gets tired. We'll get him."

The truth was I probably couldn't tire that fish out. I was fishing with my first fly rod. Now, it was a good rod to learn the basics on, but the drag system had not been designed for wearing down big fish. In fact, the drag system couldn't be tightened at all, and the way that the reel had been constructed made it nearly impossible to palm drag the spool. I knew the fish wasn't being worn down by my reel. The carp continued to casually swim close, following the little tension my rod could provide; yet, as soon as it sensed movement or saw us, it swam off. I was hooked onto a freight train with nothing holding us together but a spool of thread. Something was bound to go wrong.

Knowing the fish kept getting spooked by our presence, I started stepping backward into the field grass. I used my steps to provide tension while I held the reel handle firm, not allowing any line to be pulled from the spool. Again the carp moved closer. This time Darryl was standing sideways along the outside edge of the shallow. He stood out of the fish's path, giving the carp a free run into the muddy bank. As I continued to step backwards, the carp came into view. The fish's thick back broke the surface. Its giant scales finally exposed, Darryl and I saw exactly how big the fish was. With the carp wallowing, its belly pushing through the soft clay, its fanned-out tail slapping water across the surface; Darryl moved behind the beast and tried to trap it. Instantly the carp turned, shot toward deeper water, and ran through Darryl's straddling legs. The 8-pound leader snapped across the crotch of Darryl's khakis and the carp was free.

Darryl stared at me, dumbfounded. He probably felt responsible for the lost fish, but that carp was at least three feet long and weighed a good thirty pounds. On 8-pound test with a cheap reel and no drag, I was lucky to have fought the fish as long as I did.

"Shit!" Darryl yelled, voicing the exact emotion that was going through my head.

"I don't think there was a damn thing we could have done differently," Darryl added, baffled.

"No. We never stood a chance in hell."

Darryl stepped out of the clouded water, his legs covered in gray clay. From the knees down, he looked like a statue, his calves, ankles, and feet completely covered in the soft pond mud. He shook the water from his arms and wiped his muddy hands across his pants. I reeled in the line completely, broken leader wound loosely onto the cheap fly reel. I had no need to re-tie. I was going home.

Darryl picked up his rod and walked along the dusty trail back around the pond toward the fishing hole he had left when he came to help. He was carrying one sneaker and two balled-up, mud-covered socks in one hand and a limber fly rod in the other. Darryl watched the ground, and grasshoppers shot from stalks as he brushed past. Cutting through the cattails and readying another cast, he looked more disappointed than I did. "I'm going home!" I yelled as Darryl shot his line toward the lily pads.

On the way back I took my time and walked slowly through the field. Mr. Johnston, the owner of the farm and the pond, was baling hay in the neighboring pasture. A lone crow cawed from atop a rusted plow in the middle of the cow pen. I climbed the wobbly barbed-wire fence and crossed into the thicket of trees. I stopped along the red clay path and picked muscadines from a vine tangled in the low limbs of a water oak. The sweet taste of grapes cleared my dried mouth, but the feeling of losing that fish was still sour.

Although I was disappointed, maybe even heartbroken, I think that losing that fish was part of the reason I cast to that carp for years after. Pitting my instinct against that of a monster was what fishing became. The battle was a primal competition between species, and my adversary had beaten me. I knew that water like the back of my hand and thought my knowledge would land the fish, but the carp knew Johnston Pond in a way I never could. Pictures of trophies fill my photo albums, but memories of lost fish haunt my dreams.

The next day I went back with a fresh fly knotted to a new leader and tried again. I never hooked the carp a second time, but the chance that I might kept me casting.

Floating Toward Humility

The height of the fall spawn showed in the brightness of the maples, the chill in the air, and the crimson pectoral fins that shot upstream as I sloshed through the creek. I waited for these days all year, the moments when brook trout exploded into vibrancy, the times when every shade became as vivid as wet oil paints. At best it would last two, maybe three, weeks. Then the brown color would set in, the leaves would wilt and fall, the natives would dull, and the trees would become skeletons of themselves. For now, the fish were there, I was ready, and all that separated us was a thin strip of tippet and a Royal Coachman.

The year before, I'd found a pod of spawners in the headwaters of Moses Creek. Zac and I had fished the creek from bottom to top and finally found fish at the day's end. A twenty-foot waterfall cascaded down a slender cliff face and a large open pool gathered beneath the plunge. The pool was as far as the trout could run upstream to spawn, and it seemed that every native in the creek had made the journey. Beds lined the sandy edges outside eddies, sex-driven brookies jolted around the beds, and other trouts' curving bodies were stacked in the deeper water of the main flow. We hooked at least twenty fish before we climbed a wet grapevine up the falls and found little more than a shallow trickle of the creek remaining. A few days later the fish were gone, ghosts until the next year. Now the time had come and I was back. I hiked two miles up the red clay logging road and tromped through shallows to get to good water. Ignoring likely runs and gorgeous pocket water, my mind was made up that the fish would be at the top again. I had absolutely no use for wasting time on the small water when the trout had gathered in the last hole.

My decision was a mistake. As I watched red fins take off through the ripples, I knew the fish had yet to make it all the way up the creek. My reliance on repeating the pattern of the year before had led me past miles of fish, but it was too late now to turn back and start over. I had to fish the remaining creek and hope a couple of trout had migrated to the last pool.

I'd made one of the biggest blunders that a fisherman can make—faith in repetition. I should have known that just because something works one time, or one day, doesn't mean it will work again. I've cast dry flies to fish that repeatedly rose during a caddis hatch one evening; and when I fished the same stretch the following day, I watched them roll on nymphs during the same hatch until the sun disappeared. That is not to say that I cannot learn from success, but as Heraclitus wrote, "You could not step twice in the same river; for other waters are ever flowing on to you." I should have read the water of that day, but I played out the currents of a year before. Emerson said, "A foolish consistency is the hobgoblin of little minds," and I'd been a fool.

With little more than a half-mile stretch of creek before the last hole, I found a nice run that looked promising. The shaded current flowed under the stretched boughs of a hemlock, and I had no doubt that somewhere there'd be a fish waiting. I plucked the Royal Coachmen from the cork handle of the 2-weight and rubbed Gink into the hackles. The peacock herl and red floss body shone in the afternoon sun, and I knew it was a nice attractor pattern for the shaded water. I stripped some line, began the false cast, and aimed for the head of the run. The cast had to be tight, but there was enough room to squeeze through the narrow lane outside the hemlock branches. I made the cast, and as the line shot forward, a slight turn of the wrist directed the fly into the tree. The tippet wrapped a few times around a quivering branch, and there was no use jerking. I would have to go get it.

I stepped toward the entangled branch—the tippet wrapping the fresh growth like spider web—and watched as a nice-size native swam from my encroaching footsteps. The trout had lain right where I thought, but a mistake on the cast had ruined my shot. Second chances were out of the question with these fish. I flipped the fly around the limb, the Coachmen fell to the water, and I stumbled back to the bank. With fly in hand, the crimped tippet stretched near breaking, I knew I'd have to re-tie. I plopped down onto the bank, cursed to myself, and bit through the ruined tippet. The mishap meant more time lost on a day when the sun was sinking fast, and I'd yet to even see a fish rise.

Around the forest floor where I sat, shining buckeyes were scattered like a game of marbles. I looked up into the outstretched arms of an Ohio buckeye, towering at least fifty feet. The needle-covered seed casings lay shriveled around the trunk, and the freed seeds had rolled away from the tree's base. I remembered my grandfather always carrying a buckeye in his pocket for luck and thought, what the hell…it couldn't hurt. I found a fat, auburn-colored seed with a big, tan eye along the bottom, made a socket with my thumb and index finger, and cradling the seed inside, I saw where it had gotten its name. I knew the seeds were poisonous and that the Cherokee had floated them in pools for generations in these waters to stun trout. As I dropped the buckeye into the mesh pocket of my fly vest, all I hoped was that it could bring me at least one fish. I prayed that luck could fix my mistake.

I didn't have time to dawdle, and, with a new piece of tippet and the fly re-tied, I stepped back onto the logging road. A half mile of trail led to the hole, and my only hope was that the fading light would grant me a few casts to a native brook trout. The Coachman hadn't even touched water yet, but one fish dressed up for the spawn would bring a happy end to an otherwise unfortunate trip.

Hearing the sound of water crashing on rock, I ducked beneath a thick tangle of rhododendron blocking the view of the falls and finally saw the hole. Sunlight still touched the creek's edge, and I was happy that I'd made it in time. I walked forward, stopping on a long slab of limestone to stay far enough back from the pool. I knelt down, scoped the water, and looked for movement beneath the surface. Instantly, I saw a lone native reposition itself on the sandy shallow.

I took the Royal Coachman into my fingers and stripped some line off the Fly Logic reel, the drag clicking as I pulled. I checked around me, unwilling to snag any branch on the backcast, and saw that the only tree posing a threat was a thin paper birch fifteen feet behind. I repositioned myself on the limestone so that the line would miss the limbs and began the rhythm. As soon as I lifted the rod, graphite slapped wood and leaves, and the overhanging limb shook from the impact. The trout vanished into the bubbling waterfall, and my final shot was gone as fast as it appeared.

"Son of a bitch!" My yell echoed off the granite cliff face. I'd looked everywhere but up, and my mistake had cost me. The smack of rod on limb, the rattle of leaves, and the waving branches of the tree had sounded the starter pistol for the spooked native sitting ready on the blocks. The trout was gone, the sun was dying, no more water to fish, and I hadn't gotten one drift, let alone a bite. If I'd dreamed it, I would have woken up sweaty and shaking, but at least it wouldn't have been real. Instead, I was wide awake, pissed off, and headed home with no one to blame but myself. I yanked the rod, ripping the line from the tree, the leader snapping, and the fly left dangling in the dogwood.

I marched fast down the trail toward the truck like some hopped-up SS infantryman during the Blitz. Usually I walked slowly and tried to suck in every detail, but I was livid. I saw no beauty in the world at that moment, the color of fall leaves only mocking my rage. I got to the pickup, chucked the rod in the bed, didn't even bother taking off my waders, and spun tires all the way down the gravel road. I threw a grown man hissy fit.

I know it was immature, but it was a shitty day, a day when nothing had gone right, a slate I'd just as soon wipe clean. They say the sun shines on a dog's ass every once in a while, but that day I was not that dog, and I sped toward a case of cold beer with the pedal mashed beneath my muddy wading boot. A long time passed before I took anything away from that trip besides a hangover, a scratched reel, and bad memories; but maturity never comes easily.

Thinking back on that day, my blood still boils a little, but eventually my heart rate settles and I laugh. The truth is I've never learned anything when every cast went perfectly. I seem to learn more about myself during my darkest hours than I ever do during the short-lived seconds of perfection, and as I've grown older these are the times I value most.

Now, my eyes instinctively check every angle before I lift my rod to cast, a habit I wouldn't have picked up without days spent tangled in trees. That's not to say that I don't get mad when I watch a fly wrap high on a limb, but I calm more quickly now.

Fishing one afternoon with my dad on the Catawba in late fall, I let my anger ruin one of the few moments we got to share on the water anymore. My first five casts wrapped the limbs of a crabapple, and every time I jerked, the line snapped, and my bobber was left bouncing in the tree. Cold rain began pelting the boat and fueled my rage. The scene was like some pastoral elegy for the death of my fishing ability, where the weather reflected and intensified the emotion.

I cursed, stamped, threw the spinning rod into the bottom of the boat, and sucked on a damp cigarette, the tobacco almost too wet to burn. My dad's age kept him sober, but it wasn't long before my mood destroyed our day on the river, and we headed home. That day is one of those moments I wish I could take back but can't—time lost on the water with my father—and all I can do is remember and learn.

The Royal Coachman still dangles in the dogwood on Moses Creek. Every time I hike back to that pool, the fly's rusted hook reminds me of the day I lost. The fly hangs around like the rest of my bad memories, but like them all, it has something to teach. Those moments of mistake shatter the illusion of perfection, shock me into realization that there's still room for improvement, and force me to recognize my humanity. Fishing has become one of my life's greatest teachers. Humanity is inherently flawed.

I've spent years reading the words of the great philosophers, from Plato to Nietzsche. Though their prose left me awed, their thoughts never taught me as much about life as time spent knee-deep in the water with a fly hung in the hemlocks. Just as soon as my ego grows and my head swells, there always seems to be a tree limb to knock me down a peg. Sure enough, I will make a cast right into the limbs, lose everything, and have to start from scratch. Older now, I try to inhale deeply, use my breathing as meditation, collect myself, accept my imperfections, and re-tie.

In early February the recent snowmelt had the Tuckasegee racing high along its banks. Grassy shorelines that had remained yellow, bringing a shot of color to an otherwise dead season, were now bowed beneath the rising current. The memory of a handful of winter browns I'd caught a few weeks earlier brought me back to the icy river again. I'd readied my fly box with midge patterns and tied a couple dozen Zebra Midges and Brassies. The browns had hammered Brassies and Zebras before and I hoped—but did not expect—to find them again.

I eased the truck onto the shoulder, grabbed my vest and rod from the bed of the pickup, and walked down a gravel path to the riverside. My waders were layered over sweat pants and a thermal shirt, and my Hodgeman boots were laced tight. Choosing comfort over the harsh reality of winter, I'd heated myself in the thermostat-controlled warmth of my apartment, and, as wind hissed across the water, I was glad that I had.

I rummaged through my vest and found my midge box, loaded with flies ranging from size 18 to 26. Eying the rows of flies, I plucked a Zebra Midge and Brassie from the white foam. My shivering fingers, stinging red, made it hard to run line through the tiny hook eyes. I must have lost two or three flies along the bank as I struggled to hold onto them. Twenty-twenty vision was barely enough to see the thin-wire hooks, but I managed and eventually got the miniscule patterns on the line.

I knew that the flies, weightless in my palm, would not be able to get down to the bottom in the raging current. So I grabbed some tin shot and pinched them into place, sixteen inches up the tippet. I hoped the weight would help get the flies bouncing on the bottom where midges belonged.

I stepped into the water. The chill didn't immediately make it through my leather Hodgemans, neoprene booties, and layered socks, but I knew that it wouldn't take long. Standing on grass covered by rising water, I stripped some line off of the reel and made a short cast into the middle of the river. The line, leader, and flies were swiftly yanked downstream without having even a chance of sinking. Water seethed too quickly to allow the midges to get deep, so I added a little more shot.

Venturing a little farther out, I cast toward an eddy formed by a fallen tree on the far bank. The midges and shot plopped in, but again the line was pulled downriver and the flies rose to the surface like skiers being towed by a jet boat. No amount of mends, or even a tuck cast for that matter, could get the midges deep. Back on the bank, I rethought the situation, bit the tippet above the flies, opened my fly cases, and settled on an olive Woolly Bugger with lead wire wrapped heavy beneath the chenille. I didn't know if the large streamer would catch a wintertime trout but surely it would sink.

The heavy fly tugged at the backcast, the rhythm slowed by the weight of the Bugger. The fly struck the surface and then sank into the dark water. Ripping line from the reel and wiggling it through the tip-top, I dead-drifted the streamer to keep the path along the far side of the seam. As fast as I could get line off the reel, the current took the floating line. I could barely keep up but, with the drag loosened, managed to get a fairly straight drift. The fly began to sweep back as it moved downstream, eventually swinging directly below me. I stripped in the Bugger, the yellow glitter in the olive-colored chenille sparkling beneath the sheen, and watched as it came over the sunken grass in short hops. The fly was heavy enough to bounce the bottom now where the trout would lay, but after a few more casts and no bites, I moved further up the river.

Making my way through tangled underbrush—the twigs, vines, and briars harder and more brittle in winter—I found a small patch of ground still edging over the high-water mark. Carefully, I stepped down a short embankment, my knees beginning to tighten from the cold, until I stood on the tiny island of mud, rocks, and dead leaves. My boots sank, bubbles gurgling up from beneath my felts, and I scoped out the river.

Where a line of stones created a nice run in low water, a rapid now rolled over on itself, surely spinning stones along the bottom.

The water pushed against a sandy peninsula across the stream, and a large pool eddied out on the backside. If I could catch that line bending around the strip of sand, I was certain that a trout, conserving energy in calmer water, would be sitting there. The cast would be tough, but good placement and dead-drifting fast might catch the right current.

I began a side-armed cast, the Bugger shooting parallel to the naked limbs along the bank. At the very last moment, with just enough line to cover the distance, I changed direction; the hook sank into a limb, the tippet popped, and the line fell lifeless into the current. I breathed deeply, tried to hold in my disgust, bit my tongue, and grabbed the Bugger box from the back of my vest. This time I chose yellow chenille with brown hackle and tied the fresh fly onto the tippet.

I tried a roll cast, but the weight of the streamer kept me from building any distance, and the fly came nowhere close to the seam. The Bugger was sucked into the small hydraulic, spun beneath the rapid, and then slung downstream.

With no way to get a decent cast, I decided to risk the current to get a better chance at the drift I wanted. Stepping off the small patch of earth, I immediately felt the rush of water, only calf-high, pushing against my legs. Still too close to the shoreline for any type of backcast, I attempted another roll cast. This time it landed a bit farther out but still a good ten feet from where I needed.

I inched a few feet further into the current, careful to keep my feet solid on the freestone bottom, and the water quickly rose above my knees, thigh-high. I had just enough room to try a standard backcast, but as the Bugger tipped trees, I could shoot no more line, and my cast still fell short. I was determined to get one good drift along the far side and hopefully catch a seam that would curve the streamer back into the slack water, so I pushed a bit deeper.

My feet were unstable now, and I bent my knees a tad to steady my stance. The current pushed around my waist; I made the cast, still short, and the felts began to lose their grip. I shifted for sturdiness, decided that a cast wasn't worth being sucked downriver, and reeled in the wet Bugger. I felt stable now but thought it better to give up on the fish than to be dunked into a February snowmelt.

Facing downstream, I started to sidestep toward shore, but as I did, my planted foot began to rise from the stone it was holding to. My other foot was already off the bottom. I was a goner. As my right foot continued to come up in the current, I went down, my loose-fitting waders ballooning up like parachute pants while icy water wrapped around my legs. I gasped, panicked, and tried to scream; but no sound came out. I was breathless, and who would hear me anyway? My legs rose in the current as I floated downstream, my head barely above water, the fly rod thrashing in my right hand. I bumped against rocks and clawed at their slick sides, but I could not get a grip. I was moving too quickly to grab onto anything. My head continually went under—frigid water running into my nose each time I was dunked, the overcast sky hazier each time I broke the surface with water stinging my eyes, my ears ringing. I thought I was surely drowning.

I was pulled fifty yards downriver before I managed to get a breath. At that moment, I could either fight the river or let the current take me away. Somehow, through panicking thoughts, I realized struggling would do nothing, so I surrendered myself to the river and floated toward humility. Only when I surrendered did I find an escape. As the felt soles of my wading boots caught rock, I stood up with the freezing water waist-high in my waders, and trembled toward the shoreline. Finally safe, I laughed through shivers and gasps. The truck was in sight, but it was hard to move. My body was frozen. I walked hunched over like an old woman shaking from age and got to the truck. Water sloshed around my legs as I started the engine, cranked up the heat, and revved the motor. Soaked, I stripped the drenched clothes from my body, threw them in the back, and climbed in the cab barefoot and with nothing but dripping boxers on my body. I had nothing dry.

That day nothing went right: the current was too fast, the water was too high, my casts were too short, and the flies were too light. Through the onset of hypothermia, I drove toward home. My flesh was on fire and it felt like needles were piercing my contracted muscles, but surprisingly, I never stopped smiling. The truck didn't warm for five miles, and the entire time my body shook, my hands turning white as they clenched the steering wheel. The river had shown me who was boss. The water couldn't be tamed. I was the intruder and I was human. I was helpless against the force of the wild. It didn't matter what I'd come for; it didn't matter how much I respected its power. I left cold and wet, and the river continued to rise.

Tailout

The river was low as I walked down a gravel driveway to the hole below Webster Bridge. Overcast skies kept the summer sun from baking me, but there was still enough light to see clearly through the glassy water. The driveway hugged the bend of the Tuckasegee, but off the left side of the dirt, a steep embankment booby-trapped with groundhog holes dropped down to the still water of the pool. A mist seemed to be hovering over the current, but the cloud didn't sit like fog. The mist moved in a single horde, a silvery smoke of wings—a caddis hatch.

I stopped along the edge of the embankment and sat down on a cedar stump, the red wood smooth and weathered. From the tailout, through the pool, up the head, and disappearing behind trees in full foliage, the swarm of caddisflies hovered just above the moving water. The hatches usually didn't get this thick until evening, but the cool air of a dreary day had sprung the bugs into flight.

A groundhog wobbled through the tangled hillside, stopped, looked up at me, then began chewing kudzu from a vine, the leaves vanishing behind the furry rodent's yellowed teeth. I looked back to the river and watched as ripples began to appear chaotically across the flat surface. It had to be rain, but a drop had yet to touch my sun-tanned arms, and I heard no sound among the leaves. The movement was trout, steadily sipping flies from the surface, as the egg-laying caddisflies dropped and held a bit too long.

I began to see the silhouettes come up from the freestone bottom. The trout rose smoothly, tipped their noses through the water's edge, opened their mouths just enough to suck in wings and body, then vanished into the scattered stones. The fish were merely shadows, indistinguishable until they fed and disappeared. Mesmerized, I couldn't move.

My rod lay on the green grass beside me, dew still dotting the blades, the sweet smell inhaled on every breath I took. I'd come to fish, but marveling at the sight, I was paralyzed. A breeze hissed through the leaves, the sound softened by the freshness of new growth, and still the flies continued to come. The swarm was a river above the stream, the currents moving in opposite directions. The wings never ventured farther than the water's edge, as the caddisflies followed every bend, nook, and run of the water. I stared into a rhythm beyond any I'd ever seen; everything in tune—wings, fins, wind, water—all keeping time. The rhythm was the music of the world.

A large trout flew through the surface at the tailout of the hole. It had been keeping a line along the sandy inside of the bend. The trout's eyes were fixated on the movement above and had spotted a meal. The monster had exploded instinctively and had broken the stillness, fed, and belly-flopped against the stream. As the ripples faded away, the water stilled again. The swallowed caddis was nothing to the swarm. The fly was unnoticed by anything but the fish and would not be remembered. The feeding continued, and I watched the whole scene, not focusing on any particular spot or on any single movement but on the larger picture.

The pool was meditative chaos. Things were happening all around, too quickly to take in, the feeling like the rush of stars when one is hit hard in the head and all goes black. I fell into a dreamlike state, my eyes still watching the movement, but my mind wandering somewhere else. Staring into the sheen, I was looking into a reflection of myself. My life was flowing in front of my eyes, and for one of the first times, I kept still enough to watch it.

My home is on the water. This is the place where I belong, the place where things make sense, the place where I learn what it is to live. I was born into a family of fishermen, a group of souls whose hands were imprinted into the cork of their rods. They took me to the shoreline when I was a child. I stood at the river's edge at the high-water mark of my life and walked away a man. Nothing has taught me more and, as I daydreamed above the Tuckasegee that day, I continued to learn what the water had to teach.

On the water I met my father: not literally, but in the sense that I first met the *real* Billy Joy—not an accountant, not a choir member at the Methodist Church—but my dad. Trolling through the same river, in the Piedmont of North Carolina, where he'd learned who he was, we anchored parallel to the mud bank. Before long, Dad set the hook into a channel catfish that had swum into the shallows for a taste of bream. His flimsy spinning rod doubled over to the water as the cat tried to tug under the boat. I grabbed the net, wrapped the nylon seine around the thrashing fish, and hefted the catch up onto the carpeted bottom.

On hands and knees, Dad untangled the fish's boney pectoral fins from the net and lifted the catfish into the air. He stared over the long bluish body, the fat belly sinking down like a sack of potatoes, and then looked up at me. At that moment, I saw him. I watched the anxiety of taxes, bills, and work melt away in his eyes. All that was left was the man, a fifty-year-old man who grinned like a child as he held the six-pound channel cat.

The Catawba River, with its muddy water the color of chocolate milk, was our family river. We were students of the wild, and each one in our family had come and each had learned. The deeper the water, the deeper the stories, our ancestors beneath the current, beneath the vanishing light, beneath the clay bottom, buried in our blood.

Before us, there was Granny, and before her, her father, and before him another fisherman, his rod fitted to his hand just like ours. Granny used to sit me on her lap and tell me stories of the river before my time, when the river was still untapped. She'd share tales of jon boats, fish fries, trophy catches, family trips, and heritage. Through those stories, I learned my ancestry and the importance of continuing the line; because our family, much like rivers, had to keep moving.

A week into the summer after I graduated college, Granny lay struggling in a hospital bed. She asked me not to leave her, so I stayed. My sister, Deana, and I stood beside the bed that night, the smell of sterilization enveloping the room. Needles stuck into Granny's hands and lines ran from her body into the machines she was hooked to. She kept asking about the music and who the other people in the room were, but it was just us three. During a brief moment of clarity, Alzheimer's having left little of the woman I loved, Granny took me by the hand, pulled me close, and whispered, "I'll leave you stories."

Staring down at her hand, the large blue veins running beneath her fragile skin like the rivers we fished, I knew exactly what she meant. The things I remember most (besides being wrapped in her arms or casting next to her along the shore of the Outer Banks) are the stories, stories that echoed days on the water, stories that changed my life.

One of my favorite photographs shows her standing with me on the beach at the water's edge. She's wearing a pastel yellow shirt and matching shorts, with a straw hat tied tight under her chin with a piece of white ribbon. I'm only knee-high to a coon dog, but she's handing me the rod. She's looking down and telling me something I can't remember, probably some syllables filled with wisdom that I'm too young to fully grasp. I have no idea what the words were, but I know that they are embedded in the man I've become.

Eventually, I drifted away from the trails my family had cut to the river. I chose my own path, my own water, my own fish, but I continue what they started. When my first friend committed suicide, I grieved on the banks of the Catawba. When another friend did the same a year later, I stared into the open casket and remembered a time we shared on the water. I'd taken him to Johnston Pond, and we'd caught a feisty catfish under the light of a full moon. He'd been happy. I left the funeral parlor alone, just as I'd come. I drove to the river and fished for channel cats all night while my tears turned the fresh water brackish. At every milestone, there is a story of water, of fish, and, most importantly, of life.

In my favorite section of *Walden*, Thoreau writes that, "[he] went to the woods...to front only the essential facts of life, and see if [he] could not learn what it had to teach, and not, when [he] came to die, discover that [he] had not lived." My family has done the same, and we have all grown to adulthood surrounded by water. What I've come to understand at this juncture of my journey is that the greatest courage is simply to live. "Simplicity, simplicity, simplicity."

It's as if I were born into the head of a giant pool, rushed into the hole by current, and beaten against rocks as the rapids rolled over themselves. When I'd come to learn what was there, I was spit through the tailout, and forced downriver, only to repeat it all again. At times, the water choked me and held me beneath the current too long, but as I came up, gasping for breath, I found life.

I imagine the words Granny told me when the photograph was taken, and what I hear are words from a Flannery O'Connor story: "Everything that rises must converge." Our rivers are transcendental, eventually merging in one place, unknown and unseen until we get there. Once we are there, we find that the prize wasn't the destination; all that mattered was the journey. In the currents, I find a place where I belong, a flow that is swift, but sweet. And through the tail-out, there are stories worth telling, fading memories, and glimpses of lives well-wasted.

When I emerged from my trance below Webster Bridge, the trout were still rising. The caddisfly hatch had not slowed very much, but the clouds were beginning to break. The August sun shot beams across the shimmering river, and the ghostlike fish became more visible through the glints. I could see the trout repositioning themselves along the rocks. They took lines for food and jolted back and forth to steady themselves in the current.

I stood up from the cedar stump, my knees tight from the long meditation, and grabbed my rod from the grass. The clouds separated quickly, and humidity came on heavy as the sun evaporated the trapped moisture. I walked farther down the gravel driveway to a place where the embankment lowered onto a small piece of flat land. Mockernut hickories shaded the ground, and large granite boulders stuck up from the passing river.

I leaned against the largest rock, the smooth stone cool through my T-shirt and vest, then took out a fly box full of gray Goddard Caddisflies that I'd tied to match the dissipating hatch. After running line through the guides, I knotted a couple onto the tippet. Flies still danced across the smoky surface, but most of the caddis had vanished quickly into the trees.

Trout still came up, taking the few bugs that remained, but I found it hard to believe that what I'd seen had happened. Perhaps I'd dreamed it all. The moment had come and gone so quickly that

I'd barely had time to fully grasp the revelation, to nearly hold it in my hand. That brief glimpse was a dandelion seed that landed for an instant in my mind, but the wind had taken it away as I tried to focus. That seems to be the way revelation comes—there one second and gone the next.

The big trout leapt from the same spot again, this time contorting its body as it slapped back through the surface. Closer now, I could see that it was the giant brown. The fish solidified the events that had taken place, but it didn't matter. I'd learned what the river had to teach and for that I was thankful.

I stepped into the stream, the current sweeping around my boots as I stood on a sunken slab of granite. The flies dangling from my rod were mirror images of the few caddisflies that remained, but I could not find it in myself to make the cast to the brown. I was too connected at that point, far too attached to the place to disturb it. So I just stood there and watched.

I am a man defined by fish, a fisherman who has begun to grow gills, whose name is written in water. I wanted nothing more than to see what the world was like from beneath the current, to gaze up at tiny bodies silhouetted by the sun. I wanted to break the surface like the trout, gain a perspective of the dry world for a moment, and then return to the wet. I was blessed to have found the place where I truly belonged but cursed to know it was a place I could never fully join. I had to accept my humanity but would spend my entire life trying to get as close to the river as I could.

I knew as long as I could hear the sound of water, I could find my way home. I stared at the river in front of me, the pool curving around the bend, the trout still mouthing ripples, but I didn't make a cast. I'd seen what I was meant to see, and it was beautiful. I turned downstream and looked at the water stretched out in front of me. Time to move farther downriver, I thought. Miles of water I'd yet to wade meandered through the valley. I walked away from the tailout to find the next hole on the river and had no doubt, when I arrived at that place, I'd know it.